Something Out of *Nothing*

Paul Snyder
author/editor

Compact Library Publishers™
Copyright 1988 – 2020
All Rights Reserved
Cover Image Curtesy NASA

838 E High St #130
Lexington, Ky 40502
CLiP@ws5.com

Version 2

There is a profound difference between concluding that on my physical death all that will remain is my past, and in concluding that on my physical death all will be as if it never was.

First Things First

Something Out of *Nothing* evolved over some forty years from a short essay to this small book. It is basically a supplement to our online and eBook philosophy-religion essays (http:\\www.LifeNotes.org)[1] in which we engage in a quest for what many think they have already found, and what others think is a futile goal, the meaning of life. Complete understanding of our existence is indeed an unreachable goal because we are a small part of the universe. Unless the whole reveals its true nature to a part, the part can never fully understand the whole. Yet we, along with most people, believe that the journey itself leads to wisdom and is worth embracing. We do not pretend to have special knowledge that will be revealed to you, we do however think that we can focus your attention on an intuitive understanding of human existence.

We discuss what continues to be a popular idea, existential meaning. Indeed, the quest for a scientific foundation for philosophy from which existentialism might evolve has led to renewed interest in naturalism, which the philosopher Owen Flanagan calls "the only game in town".[2] The broad definition of existential we adopt in this book states that life has meaning and purpose *in and of itself.* In our modern, increasingly secular, world we often ignore the question of whether there is a meaning and purpose for our lives.

Pragmatic thinkers may not recognize a need to search for a universal reason for living, and may accept without question an

---

[1] Mirror site www.ws5.com

[2] Owen Flanagan and Gregg D. Caruso, "Neuroexistentialism," *The Philosophers' Magazine* (2018): accessed December 20, 2019, https://www.philosophersmag.com/essays/194-neuroexistentialism

existential belief that life is simply to be lived. The primary purpose of our discussion is to explore the rationality of such a belief in light of our finite physical existence. We present a logical argument which suggests that the foundation of humanism is irrational. In our other books and essays we look for a reason for living.

We will explore birth, physical existence, and eventual death, not as a morbid exercise, but rather to challenge you to think about the possible consequences of accepting life as is, without critical evaluation of what it means to be human. We will try to make sense of the great number of academic ideas about what it means to live and die. If we are successful, when you finish this book you will have a better appreciation of what it means to be human and what the consequences of your choices may be.

In previous shorter essays our approach was to rely on the reader's independent inquiry and common sense to evaluate our claims. In this book we offer a bit more contemplative tone, with references to academic materials we believe support our methodology and conclusions. If you read the additional materials you will have a good overview of the current (2020) state of the topics. If you enjoy looking at the condition of human knowledge in the third millennium, you will want to read as many of the referenced works as time allows.

We face the problem that our inquiry is broad, and that to do justice to centuries of scholarly work and the ongoing debates would require an encyclopedia. To shorten the task ahead we will often, rather disjointedly, jump from topic to topic, leaving the reader to explore the references. By doing so we do not believe that we are glossing over serious objections to our conclusions.

Before moving forward we should better define our goals so that the path we take might seem a little less rambling. While there are innumerable variations of almost every philosophical and scientific argument, we focus on what intuitively appear to be the most promising options.[3] We leave extreme theories to

---

[3] Intuition in both the traditional sense of unexplained knowledge and the more scientific sense as in Andrzej Piotr Wierzbicki, "Rational and

others, only briefly considering remote possibilities such as ontological nihilism[4] - the argument that nothing exists. That is not to say that we will not delve into the nature of *nothing*,[5] which is one of our primary concerns. But we will not spend time arguing whether or not "I am a figment of your imagination."[6]

> **An important warning!** There is a risk that as you read this book you may think we are suggesting that *nothing* may await us after our physical death and that therefore there is no meaning in life. That is not what we are saying at all. In fact we are saying the opposite, we believe that if you understand what is said you will be able to find in yourself the reason for living. If you become fearful or depressed as you consider our ideas you simply do not understand what we are saying. There is absolutely no reason to be fearful or troubled or even concerned by our arguments or conclusions. If you are discouraged, please finish reading all of this book including the last chapters, and perhaps our other books, where we explain why there is no logical reason for any negative thoughts. Anyone who is, or becomes, seriously depressed should always seek immediate medical help. If you are distressed by our ideas please read the Appendix at the end of our book.

Evolutionary Technical Theory of Intuition." In *Technen: Elements of Recent History of Information Technologies with Epistemological Conclusions* (New York: Springer International Publishing, 2015), 79-96.

[4] Jason Turner, "Ontological Nihilism," In *Oxford Studies in Metaphysics*, ed. Karen Bennett and Dean W. Zimmerman, vol. 6, (Oxford: Oxford University Press, 2011), 3-54.

[5] When we italicize *nothing* we are referring to the fundamental nature of nothing.

[6] Gusteau to Rémy in the 2007 Pixar film "Ratatouille". Trivia, we believe that the quote "figment of your imagination" was originally made famous by Daffy Duck (figament), but that reference is lost to posterity.

3

A large amount of the text mirrors chapters in our other books, if you have read them please excuse the repetition. If you decide to read them in the future you can skip the early chapters and start in those books with the chapter - Truth, Belief, and Faith. Toward the end of this book we discuss what may be our most important contribution to the conversation of life, what *nothing* really means for those who seek something.

One last preparatory comment. We will carry with us on this journey a smooth, oval, imaginary river stone. It is just a stone, however if you were around in the 1970's you may choose to think of it as your pet rock. It may prove useful to ground our intellect during overly academic arguments.

Life and Death

At least half of Benjamin Franklin's wisdom was true when he said, "In this world nothing can be said to be certain, except death and taxes."[7] If there is anything in life we can count on occurring without fail, it is physical death. The successful bank president, the champion athlete, the housewife, the famous, the unknown, every human being, you, I, die. While all acknowledge the certainty of their eventual demise, few think about death until they are faced with it. The simple fact of death is not news to anyone, yet the reality of its impending occurrence is ignored by virtually every living person.

The very nature of human life denies death and shrouds it in the cloak of future events, events that are not yet real and need not be dealt with in the present. Living is too important and time consuming to be concerned with mortality. The fact that you are moving steadily toward your death is most likely, and literally, to be the last thing on your mind.

Our primary inquiry is who are we during our physical lives and what, if anything, will we become when we die? First, we need to ask what does it mean to be human and alive? The most unique characteristic of human beings seems to be that we perpetually make conscious choices between alternatives. All agree that we must be conscious, sentient, beings to make choices, but what does it really mean to be alive, to be conscious? We need to set the stage by looking at methods of inquiry which we have some degree of confidence will help us reach valid conclusions.

---

[7] Benjamin Franklin, *The Complete Works of Benjamin Franklin* (Lennox: HardPress Publishing, 2012).

The Search for Truth

If a scientist, philosopher, or anyone else tells you something is true,[8] and it is in fact false, then it is not true. If they tell you something is false, and it is in fact true, then it is true. To say something is true or false does not make it true or false.[9] Even though you are told something is true, if it is not true it is simply not true. On the other hand, if something is true it is true, even if you are told or believe that it is not.[10]

If something is true or false, it is true or false whether we believe it to be true or false, or have not thought about its truth at all.[11] If we believe a lamp is on a table, whether we have any evidence it is or not, and the lamp is in fact on the table, then what we believe to be true is true. If we cannot determine whether or not the lamp is on a table that does not change the actual position of the lamp. Even though without evidence we cannot prove a lamp is on a table, if it is on the table then it is on the table and our belief is true.

Just because we cannot prove something is true does not in any way mean it is not true. Yet we might ask, if there is no one in a forest to hear a tree fall, does the sound of the tree falling really exist? If there is no one to see a tree fall, does it really fall at all?[12]

---

[8] Michael Patrick Lynch, ed., *The Nature of Truth: Classic and Contemporary Perspective* (Cambridge: MIT Press, 2001).
[9] Philip Kitcher, *The Advancement of Science-Science without Legend, Objectivity without Illusions* (Oxford: Oxford University Press, 1995).
[10] María J. Frápolli, "The Neutrality of Truth in the Debate Realism vs. Anti-Realism." In *The Realism-Antirealism Debate in the Age of Alternative Logics* (Houten: Springer Netherlands, 2012), 85-99.
[11] "so long as we think of our utterances as being about something(s), there is no escape from the realist truth formula" in William P. Alston, "Yes, Virginia, There is a Real World," *The American Philosophical Association Centennial Series* (2013): 625-646 at 645. doi:10.5840/apapa2013287 – also available at JStor.
[12] Henry P. Stapp, *Mindful Universe: Quantum Mechanics and the Participating Observer* (New York: Springer Science & Business Media, 2011).

"Does an event occur if there are no observers?" is a valid question that perhaps can be answered yes only if the observer not only sees the event,[13] but also continues to exist forever beyond the time of the event. In other words, if only inanimate objects surround an event such as the turning on of a lamp, perhaps it can be said no event has occurred since nothing has been seen, heard, etc., to change.[14] Similarly, if a living observer witnesses an event but at some later date the observer ceases to exist, what value was the observation?

Of course the argument can be made that seen or not seen photons stream from a light when it is turned on. Furthermore, it can be suggested that once seen or heard an event has in some sense "actualized".[15] Much depends on how you define "event", but underlying the question is a troublesome perception that goes beyond semantics, a feeling that a world without permanent observers lacks anything similar to what we call reality.

Even though we disagree, some philosophers have moved toward the view that language is the unique factor which gives humans the ability to think thoughts, and that language is the only thing that distinguishes us from animals. They suggest that using language, our consciousness assigns the concepts of true and false to the things and events that surround us.[16] Some of them believe that truth has no meaning outside the human mind, and therefore,

---

[13] M. L Clarke, "Emerging Interpretations of Quantum Mechanics and Recent Progress in Quantum Measurement," *European Journal of Physics* 35, no. 1 (2014): 015021. doi:10.1088/0143-0807/35/1/015021

[14] Subhash Kak, Deepak Chopra, and Menas Kafatos. "Perceived Reality, Quantum Mechanics, and Consciousness," *Cosmology*, 18 (2014): 231-245. http://cosmology.com/ConsciousTime107.html

[15] Sheldon Goldstein. "Quantum Theory Without Observers," *Physics Today* 51, no. 3 (1998): 42-47. http://www.math.rutgers.edu/~oldstein/papers/qtwoe/qtwoe.html

[16] W. V. Quine, "Relativism and Absolutism," *The Monist* (1984): 293-296; Richard Rorty, *Objectivity, Relativism, and Truth: Philosophical Papers. Vol. 1.* (Cambridge: Cambridge University Press, 1991).

in a very real sense truth does not exist as an independent reality.[17]

We are not uncomfortable with the idea that in an inanimate universe truth may not exist, and therefore there must be an observer for truth to have meaning.[18] However we are very uncomfortable with the suggestion that where a permanent observer does exist, truth is merely a creation of that observer's consciousness. If we have a non-physical side to us, we may well have a perpetual consciousness that can observe and perhaps remember the truths which surround us. Whether or not a lamp has been observed to be on a table, if the lamp is physically sitting on the table the very existence of permanent observers who could observe the lamp may give independent meaning to the statement that it is true that the lamp is on the table.[19]

If memories of human events die with each person, then events themselves become little more than transient observations made by the living. Yet if we survive the grave it would seem that we would have a continuing consciousness that recognizes a real and fundamental difference between that which is true and that which is false. For now, even if you do not believe in a non-physical consciousness after physical death, please accept the possibility that some things may be either fundamentally true, or not.

If we want to consider in greater detail the nature of reality, we need to be able to make statements we can believe to be true. In our quest to find meaning in life, we must develop some method of determining truths which we can have a fair degree of confidence in. To do so we need to understand what it means to be able to prove something, scientifically or otherwise.

We will first look at our topics from the perspective of science. We will then revisit them from a philosopher's viewpoint.

---

[17] Michael Dummett, *Truth and Other Enigma* (Cambridge: Harvard University Press, 1978).

[18] George Jaroszkiewicz, "Contextual Completeness and a Classification Scheme for Theories." *arXiv preprint arXiv:1501.02961* (2015). http://arxiv.org/pdf/1501.02961v1.pdf

[19] William P. Alston, *A Realist Conception of Truth* (Ithaca: Cornell University Press, 1996).

While we favor a scientist's objectivity, the reader should be aware of the strengths and weaknesses of both approaches.

Science and the Scientific Method

Over the centuries the quest for truth has been refined into the process of scientific analysis.[20] A brief summary of what has come to be known as the scientific method is helpful.[21] Scientists observe what they want to study and record properties they believe to be relevant to their research. While some may have preconceived notions of what they will find, others begin the process of experimentation and observation without any idea what, if anything, they will discover. Even though they may believe they will achieve a certain result, scientists who do not approach every experiment with open minds are not scientists at all.

After gathering what they consider to be enough information about an object or event, scientists sit back, study the data, and try to combine and organize the information to discover a pattern running through it. They look for a model that not only describes what they currently observe, but that also perfectly matches past observations. The resulting descriptions of the world around them are known as theories or theorems. These in turn can be used to predict what will happen in the future under the same or similar circumstances.[22]

Efforts to formulate theorems that describe observations would be in vain if the universe was made up of random events, occurring without reason or order, for then no one could say what

---

[20] G. Ellis and J. Silk, "Scientific Method: Defend the Integrity of Physics," *MNASSA: Monthly Notes of the Astronomical Society of South Africa* 74 (vol. 1 and 2) (2015): 15-21 [controversial viewpoint stresses objective experimentation before hypothesis satisfies scientific method]; P. Woit, *Not Even Wrong: The Failure of String Theory and The Search for Unity in Physical Law*, (New York: Basic Books, 2006) [We are less harsh than Woit on the possible validity of string theory].

[21] Robert Nola and Howard Sankey, *Theories of Scientific Method: An Introduction* (New York: Routledge, 2014).

[22] Stephen Carey, *A Beginner's Guide to Scientific Method* (Independence, KY: Cengage Learning, 2011).

will happen next. Of course, that appears not to be the case, as our universe seems to behave in a more or less ordered manner. As we have studied the cosmos in more and more detail, it seems to be true that all physical objects comprised of matter and energy (which may or may not include human consciousness), from the tiniest atomic particle to the largest system, behave according to some fixed set of laws.[23] These laws can be thought of as if-then statements, which describe what will happen if a certain event occurs. For example, one of the well-known results of the law of gravity is that IF an apple comes loose from the branch of a tree, THEN it will fall to earth.

For several reasons we regret using simplistic examples to make a point. Because of their simplistic nature, they tend to lessen the importance of the point being made. They narrow the reader's focus from the broad, general truth of a statement to a specific, small part of the whole. Simple examples tend to be incredibly inadequate when used to illustrate complex feelings, beliefs, and ideas. Some people feel they are being talked down to, or think they already understand what is being said. They risk missing the deep significance that often hides within the example.

On the other hand, simple examples can be used to bring a point quickly home, allowing us to bypass a good bit of background discussion and to explore at once concepts which are best understood when drawn rapidly and simultaneously into the mind. The dangers of simplistic examples can only be overcome by the reader who is aware of the shortcomings, and is willing to expand the examples in their mind so that the "profound" will not be misunderstood to be "simple".

Back to gravity and the falling apple. The law itself basically states that objects exert a force on each other which attracts them toward one another, the strength of the attraction being related to their masses and the distance between them (in

---

[23] J. Brockman, *Universe: Leading Scientists Explore the Origin, Mysteries, and Future of the Cosmos* (New York: Harper Perennial, 2014).

reality gravity is very complex,[24] but for our purposes we will stick with simplified approximations). The fundamental law of gravity was described by Isaac Newton after he observed that objects that are dropped fall toward earth. By repeating his experiment over and over again, by dropping object after object, Newton gained confidence what he theorized to be true was true, objects attract each other with a strength directly proportional to their masses and inversely proportional to the distance between them.

Each successful test of Newton's theory of gravity made scientists increasingly confident the theorem was correct. Why should repeated successes, i.e. more and more apples falling off trees, increase the confidence of the scientists? Beyond the "common sense" feeling that repeated successes increase confidence in success, is there some scientific reason to be optimistic?

Statistics

Enter the world of statistics. Mathematicians have long recognized that the larger the sample that is taken from a group of items, the better able they are to predict what individual items are like in the group. The larger the sample the more confident they can be that a strange or uncharacteristic item will not be found. This is true due to the fundamental nature of the mathematics behind statistical inference.[25] It is true no matter what the items being sampled are, so long as the sample is not biased.

---

[24] George Gamow, "Gravity," *Scientific American* 204 (1961): 94-106. http://www.scientificamerican.com/article/gamow-gravity/; Raul Carballo-Rubio, Carlos Barcelo, and Luis J. Garay, "Some Not-So-Common Ideas About Gravity," (2015). http://arxiv.org/pdf/1502.04992v1.pdf

[25] And the fundamental nature of the mathematics behind science. FQXI, "Trick or Truth: the Mysterious Connection Between Physics and Mathematics." (2015). http://fqxi.org/community/forum/category/31424; M. J. Rees, *Just Six Numbers: The Deep Forces that Shape the Universe* (New York: Basic Books, 2000).

For example, if you randomly sample 500 apples out of a box containing 100,000 thoroughly mixed apples, and find not a single rotten one, a mathematician can tell you with a great degree of confidence what the chances are that none of the 100,000 apples is rotten. If you sample 1,000 apples out of the 100,000, he or she can be more certain. After inspecting 10,000 apples, he or she can be even more certain. If 5 rotten apples are found in a sample of 500, or 45 in a sample of 1,000 the mathematician can tell you how many rotten apples you are likely to find among the 100,000 apples. No matter what is in the box, whether it is 100,000 apples, 100,000 pencils, 100,000 transistors, 100,000 anything, so long as the items are uniformly mixed, anyone can tell by drawing a random sample how many of the items in the box are likely to have one or more traits in common (i.e. color, size, shape, etc.). The bigger the sample, the more accurate the prediction and the more confident the predictor.

It should be emphasized that the predictions are accurate not because of the nature of that which is being sampled, but because the mathematical relationship between the number of samples and the number of underlying items being sampled is fixed and predictable. If you draw at random four pencils from a jar containing 100 pencils, three are white, one is red, there is a certain probability that the jar contains 75% white pencils and 25% red pencils. If you draw four golf balls from a jar containing 100 golf balls, three are white, one is red, the same probability exists the jar contains 75% white golf balls and 25% red golf balls.

If the apples in our apple barrel were not uniformly mixed, and/or the sample was drawn in some organized pattern, we might get only good apples, or at least a higher number of good apples than we would otherwise. The sample would be unrepresentative of the contents of the box and useless to the mathematician. It is very, very important to realize if we take as our sample 99,999 out of 100,000 apples and find not even a single rotten one, we can be incredibly sure we are right when we predict the one apple left in the box is not rotten. None-the-less

12

when we examine the one remaining apple it may in fact be rotten!!!!![26]

One final observation, there is a subtle distinction we usually miss when using statistics. If we say that there is a 40% chance of rain and a 60% chance of sunshine, and it rains, what was and is the reality of the 40% probability of sunshine? The idea that we can predict the likelihood of rain is obviously useful, but if you schedule a picnic and it rains the 60% chance of sunshine was in a sense never "real". While it may be useful to predict the probability of an event, when the event happens the possibility of it happening is 100%, and the possibility of it not happening is 0%.[27] We realize the difference in prediction and actualization, yet the fact that an event will happen if it is going to happen, and that statistics do nothing more than make an educated guess at which events will occur, emphasizes the fact that fundamental forces rule both the events and the statistics.[28]

Positivism

A few comments on the philosophic approach to science and statistics might be helpful. Positivism[29] is the idea that assertions can be said to be rational and justified only if they can be scientifically verified, or are capable of logical or mathematical proof.[30] A positivist rejects metaphysics and theism. Logical

---

[26] D. M. Gabbay, P. Thagard, J. Woods, P. S. Bandyopadhyay, and M. R. Forster, *Philosophy of Statistics* 7 (Paris: Elsevier, 2011).

[27] K. T. Kelly, and C. Glymour, "Why Probability Does Not Capture the Logic of Scientific Justification," In ed. Christopher Hitchcock, *Contemporary Debates in the Philosophy of Science* (London: Blackwell, 2004).

[28] Andrew Gelman and Christian Hennig, "Beyond Subjective and Objective in Statistics." (2015). http://www.stat.columbia.edu/~gelman/research/unpublished/obje ctivity10.pdf

[29] Auguste Comte, *Auguste Comte and Positivism: The Essential Writings* (Livingston: Transaction Publishers, 1975).

[30] Larry Laudan and Andre Kukla. *Beyond Positivism and Relativism: Theory, Method, and Evidence* (Boulder: Westview Press, 1996).

positivism (empiricism)[31] extends the idea that cognitively meaningful statements must be verifiable either by logical reasoning or empirical experience.[32] Again metaphysical statements are not empirically verifiable and not acceptable. Logical positivism was a popular philosophy in the early 1900's, championed by Rudolf Carnap,[33] Hans Reichenbach,[34] and Karl Popper[35] (who replaced verification with falsification). At its peak of popularity[36] logical positivism was the predominant philosophy of the scientific era, but its lofty claims soon came under increasing scrutiny.[37]

The problem is that verification by experience is a dicey proposition.[38] As we will see in the next chapter, science cannot tell us that a statement is true – it can only tell us that a theory is logically consistent, and that to date experience has verified the theory and not falsified it.[39] Logical positivism was eventually discredited as a method to find absolute truth. Its fall from popularity reopened debate over the role of the metaphysical in

---

[31] Alfred Jules Ayer, ed. *Logical Positivism* (New York: Simon and Schuster, 1966); Alfred Jules Ayer, *Language, Truth and Logic,* Reprint of 1952 edition. (N. Chelmsford: Courier Dover Publications, 2012).
[32] Michael Friedman, *Reconsidering Logical Positivism* (Cambridge: Cambridge University Press, 1999).
[33] Rudolf Carnap, *The Logical Structure of the World* (Oakland: Univ of California Press, 1968).
[34] Hans Reichenbach, *The Rise of Scientific Philosophy* (Oakland: Univ of California Press, 1968).
[35] Karl Popper, *The Logic of Scientific Discovery* Reprint (London: Routledge, 2005).
[36] Moritz Schlick, Rudolf Carnap, Sahotra Sarkar, and Otto Neurath, eds. *Logical Empiricism at Its Peak: Schlick, Carnap, and Neurath* vol. 2. (London: Taylor and Francis, 1996).
[37] Hilary Putnam, *Mind, Language, and Reality* (Cambridge: Cambridge Univ. Press, 1975).
[38] James W. Garrison, "Some Principles of Postpositivistic Philosophy of Science," *Educational Researcher* 15, no. 9 (1986): 12-18. doi:10.3102/0013189X015009012
[39] Julius Rudolph Weinberg, *An Examination of Logical Positivism* (London: Routledge, 2013).

knowledge, scientific and otherwise.[40] Can science offer us knowledge of the world beyond human experience (scientific realism)[41] or is it just a human tool that predicts human experiences (instrumentalism).[42] Philosophy took several what we would call difficult turns,[43] leading to continuing debate on "objective truth".[44]

---

[40] John Earman, ed. *Inference, Explanation, and Other Frustrations: Essays in the Philosophy of Science.* vol. 14 (Oakland: Univ of California Press, 1992).

[41] John Jamieson Carswell Smart, *Philosophy and Scientific Realism* (London: Routledge, 2014).

[42] Theo Kuipers, *From Instrumentalism to Constructive Realism* (New York: Springer Science & Business Media, 2010).

[43] Hilary Putnam, "What is Realism?" In Jarrett Leplin, ed, *Scientific Realism* (Berkeley: University of California Press, 1984), 140; Margaret Archer, Roy Bhaskar, Andrew Collier, Tony Lawson, and Alan Norrie, eds. *Critical Realism: Essential Readings* (London: Routledge, 2013).

[44] Roberto Ciuni, Heinrich Wansing, and Caroline Willkommen, eds. *Recent Trends in Philosophical Logic* (New York: Springer, 2014); N. J. Pedersen, and C. D. Wright, eds. *Truth and Pluralism: Current Debates* (Oxford: Oxford University Press, 2013); N. J Pedersen, "Pluralism × 3: Truth, Logic, Metaphysics." *Erkenntnis* 79 (2014): 259-277. doi:10.1007/s10670-013-9476-x

A Law Is a Law

A law is a law until it is no longer a law. What we are building up to is the fact that the law of gravity is called a "law" because, in billions and billions of observations, not once has any documented event occurred where two objects did not attract each other in precisely the way predicted (we now know that gravity may not behave as Newton thought, but like Newton predicted, objects do move toward one another). We can say with an absolutely incredible degree of statistical certainty that the gravitational "force" between two objects will always cause them to be attracted toward one another. At this point in time there is probably less than one chance in 1,000,000,000,000,000 x 10 raised to the 1,000,000,000,000,000[th] power that gravity will not act essentially as expected. Yet, despite the incredible certainty of gravity, we do not and cannot know whether it is or is not possible for one contrary event to occur, and thus for the law of gravity to be proven wrong![45]

We are not suggesting the law of gravity is incorrect and that an event whereby it is proven wrong will ever occur. In fact we would be surprised if any of the basic scientific laws of the universe are fundamentally wrong. What we are saying is no matter how many times something has been observed to be true, no matter how incredibly unlikely it is an unexpected event will occur, we have no way of knowing if such an event is possible or impossible! If the unexpected event is not possible, it will never occur, and it will never be observed. If the event is possible, and if it does occur, then it has happened, period.

We must remember it is not the "law" which makes objects behave in a certain way, fundamental forces far beyond human comprehension do that. Rather the law describes the behavior and remains valid and true only until a single unexpected observation proves it wrong. Actually the law remains only

---

[45] A. F. Chalmers, *What Is This Thing Called Science?* (Cambridge: Hackett Publishing, 2013).

16

apparently valid and true, if it is later proven wrong its former truth was an illusion. The law was in fact always false.[46]

Modifying a theory to better fit the observations does not help render the original theory true, rather it creates a new theory that is itself either true or false. Since scientific theories are tested by observation, they are true if and only if each and every event they describe and predict, from the beginning of the universe to the end, in fact occurs exactly as expected. Theories, no matter how solid they might seem, must be discarded as false the very first time they fail to describe real events.

Observation

Science is based on observation, formulation of theories, and more observation. To observe necessarily requires the ability to perceive - to sense, feel, smell, touch, taste, see, hear. Early humans used all their senses to explore the world around them.[47] When human senses proved inadequate, they devised better and better tools and instruments to extend their range. Microscopes and telescopes to expand vision, stethoscopes and amplifiers to increase hearing, plus thousands of other sensitive devices to enhance our abilities.

The catalog of devices used to expand our human senses is enormous and growing by the minute, yet all the instruments of humankind can do no more than extend the reach of humans into the universe of which they and their instruments are a part. We know of three spatial dimensions, height, width, depth, and a fourth dimension, time (which may also prove to be spatial in nature). Space (height, width, depth), and time all exist together as space-time and cannot exist alone. Is there a fifth, a sixth, a

---

[46] Despite the excellent arguments for pluralism we prefer the idea that there is an objective truth upon which science is either forever converging, or has reached without knowledge that it has been discovered. K. T. Kelly, "Simplicity, Truth, and the Unending Game of Science." In *Infinite Games: Foundations of the Formal Sciences*, V. S. Bold, B. Loewe, T. Raesch, J. van Benthenm, eds. (Roskilde: College Press, 2007): 223-270.

[47] A. Chalmers, review of Joseph Agassi, "Creating a Social Space for Modern Science." *Metascience* 23 (2014): 173-177. doi:10.1007/s11016-013-9826-y

seventh, an eighth dimension? No one knows, for if they exist they appear (at least at this stage of human knowledge) to be separate and beyond human ability to sense, measure, and thus scientifically prove.

Does that mean those dimensions do not exist, the answer is no. Mathematicians and physicists use formulas to describe sub-atomic phenomena (e.g. string theory)[48] that can be interpreted as happening in multidimensional space. If a fifth dimension exists, it exists. If a fifth dimension does not exist, it does not exist. This is true regardless of whether we can, or never can, observe that dimension and is true for any sixth dimension, seventh dimension, eighth dimension, etc. It is important to realize that no matter how many dimensions are eventually observed, one or more additional dimensions may or may not exist beyond human ability to observe.

Many of you are saying to yourselves it is one thing to say that a dimension beyond human ability to observe may exist, but an entirely different thing to say that one probably does. You are right. Most of you will go on to say it is highly improbable, maybe less than one chance in a trillion, that even one more dimension exists beyond the observable number of dimensions, however many that may eventually prove to be. If you think that, you are wrong. To be able to statistically predict the likelihood of an event happening we must first observe to see how often the event occurs during a given period of time. If we cannot observe the event when it occurs, we cannot determine how often it happens (or conversely, does not happen) and we cannot predict the likelihood of the event.[49]

---

[48] Brian Greene, "Why String Theory Still Offers Hope We Can Unify Physics," *Smithsonian Magazine* (January 2015). http://www.smithsonianmag.com/science-nature/string-theory-about-unravel-180953637/; E. Kiritsis, *String Theory in a Nutshell* (Princeton: Princeton University Press, 2011). Lots of math.
[49] B. C. van Fraassen, "Constructive Empiricism Now." *Philosophical Studies* 106 (2001): 151-170. doi:10.1023/A:1013126824473 When we talk about something that is beyond human observation we are referring to that which is beyond even indirect observation and proof.

One problem with recognizing the limitations of statistical analysis is understanding the difference between not observing an event where the event watched for can be observed, and not observing an event where the event cannot be observed because it is beyond human ability to sense.[50] The first, not observing an event which could be seen, leads to the statistically valid conclusion that the event is unlikely to occur. The second, not observing an event which is beyond human ability to perceive, cannot lead to any conclusion at all about the reality of that event. Yet it appears to be human nature to assume that things which have never been observed do not exist, or at best are highly unlikely to exist.

If something exists beyond human perception it will never be observed during our physical lifetimes. If you cannot measure something because it is beyond human perception you cannot prove it exists, on the other hand you cannot prove that it does not exist! More importantly, you cannot say that it is statistically likely or unlikely that it exists. You simply cannot say anything objective at all about that which is beyond human ability to observe.

It is very, very important to realize that it is absolutely impossible to say that it is either likely or unlikely something exists beyond human observation. We simply cannot determine in any way the probability that something exists, or does not exist, beyond our observable universe. To understand the significance of this often overlooked statement is to understand that we have absolutely no idea what, if anything, lies beyond our cognitive boundaries.

A moments thought should bring the realization that this absolute limit of statistics and science renders all "scientific proof" and "subjective feelings" that nothing exists beyond our perception into "philosophic arguments". Despite what science

---

[50] F. A. I. Buekens, and F. A. Muller, "Intentionality Versus Constructive Empiricism." *Erkenntnis* 76 (2012): 91-100. doi:10.1007/s10670-011-9348-1; for a somewhat opposing view see - G. Contessa, "Constructive Empiricism, Observability and Three Kinds Of Ontological Commitment." *Studies in History and Philosophy of Science Part A* 37 (2006): 454-468. doi:10.1016/j.shpsa.2006.06.007

might claim to have proven, and despite what we might feel, about what lies beyond our ability to observe, we cannot say anything objective about that which is beyond human perception. We may create mathematical models of what should lie somewhere just beyond observation, yet without a means of testing these projections they can never be more than idle speculation. We simply cannot say that it is likely, or not likely, that a world or worlds exist beyond the physical universe in which we live. From an analytical standpoint anything, or *nothing*, may exist beyond human cognition.

Human beings are limited to observing the effects of fundamental forces on matter and energy, and must draw conclusions based only on such observations. We can never view the forces themselves, forces whose metaphysical existence and purpose transcend human observation and comprehension.[51] One of the consequences of being only a small part of the universe in which we live is the absolute fact that, unless revealed to us by the whole, we can never know if something or someone exists beyond the limits of our senses. No one, not you nor I nor the smartest person on earth can determine whether or not anything exists beyond that which we can observe.

The significance of the continued possibility that an unexpected event will occur to disprove even the best of theories, and the very fact such a possibility will always exist, renders it

---

[51] Some misc. comments on initial conditions and laws: Claus Kiefer, "On the Concept of Law in Physics." *European Review* 22 (2014): S26-S32. doi:10.1017/S1062798713000756; Roger Penrose, "On the Gravitization of Quantum Mechanics 2: Conformal Cyclic Cosmology." *Foundations of Physics* 44 no. 8 (2014): 873-890. doi:10.1007/s10701-013-9763-z; Stephen Wolfram, *A New Kind of Science* 5 (Champaign: Wolfram Media, 2002); Diana Battefeld, and Peter Patrick, "A Critical Review of Classical Bouncing Cosmologies." *Physics Reports* (2015); Lorenzo Battarra and Jean-Luc Lehners, "On the No-Boundary Proposal for Ekpyrotic and Cyclic Cosmologies," *Journal of Cosmology and Astroparticle Physics* 12 (2014): 023. doi:10.1088/1475-7516/2014/12/023; Lee Smolin, "Unification of the State with the Dynamical Law." *Foundations of Physics* 45, (2015): 1-10. doi:10.1007/s10701-014-9855-4 We are very skeptical of Smolin's dynamical law theory.

impossible to prove anything to be absolutely true or false. Since even the most incredibly supported laws are always subject to being disproved by the happening of a single contrary event, all laws and theorems and common sense proofs are subject to being disproved. Fundamental precepts that apples fall, water flows, fire burns, may all be disproved by future events.

Our limitations not only prevent us from exploring that which is beyond human perception, but also add to all human observations a degree of uncertainty that cannot be overcome. We can never say with total certainty that anything is true, or for that matter, untrue. In this age of science it is hard for those who have not studied the scientific method in its most intricate details to understand that, because it is a tool of human beings, it is necessarily limited in its application by the limits of human comprehension and understanding.

It is even harder to accept that, since we are only a part of the whole universe, we can never determine by ourselves what the entire universe is like. Being a part of the whole means that every law we construct must be built from unprovable assumptions, assumptions that may or may not hold true in the future. We can never know if something, or someone, outside our perception will alter all or part of what we observe, rendering untrue in an instant the very best of our proofs.

Of course, if underlying forces do exist, are not changed, and require the predicted behavior, then the laws never can and never will be disproved. However, that does not alter the fact that it is, and always will be, beyond human ability to prove anything. There is absolutely no way human beings can determine if fundamental forces exist that will never change. We simply cannot determine if it is possible, or if it is not possible, for a contrary event to occur. We can never be certain that contrary events will not happen, we can never prove that anything is absolutely true.

You Can't Believe Your Eyes

We must be sure of observations that are within the bounds of human perception, and skeptical if what we observe appears to be opposite to that which is predicted. Yet we must also be willing to recognize and accept valid experimental data that disproves popular theories. Scientists have declared many theories to be true and elevated them to the status of law, only to discover that future observations, often more accurate than the first, proved them wrong.

There are millions of examples of these errors. Perhaps the most famous was the early contention that the earth was flat,[52] a scientific "fact" based on observations that appeared sound to early scholars, and which should not be so surprising to those of us who live in hilly country without a visible horizon. What all of us, including scientists, must be aware of is the ease in which we convert our theories into laws. Even if we believe our minds are open, most of us grab onto favorite theories and assumptions. We think of, and talk about, them as though there is no doubt they are true.

We should take a minute to discuss the potentially seductive nature of misinterpreted or misused scientific proof. In the 1900's high school biology texts described the propulsion method of certain one-cell microscopic animals (protozoa) through water by declaring they waved a tail like projection back and forth. The books had been careful to label many new ideas as theories, but stated this particular description in absolute terms since these one-celled animals had been observed for many, many years always moving in exactly the same way. Anyone reading the text would believe, as scientists and everyone else did, that there was absolutely no question how the animals got around.

Watching television some ten years later I was surprised to hear of an accidental discovery by a scientist looking at some protozoa. Trying to hold one still under a microscope he held down the tail with a needle. Instead of the body of the animal thrashing back and forth as it should have, he observed it to be spinning around the tail.

The tail was attached to the body by what was in effect a small rotating joint, which acted like an electric motor spinning a

---

[52] A few remaining flat-earth believers think that the Earth is a disc whose center is at the North Pole. Around the edge there is a wall of ice that prevents the oceans from flooding over the border.

propeller.[53] Looking more closely, the scientist discovered the tail was in fact shaped like a corkscrew. Because the microscopic view had always been two dimensional, rather than three, the corkscrew motion looked down on from above had appeared to be that of a wave.

Since it was common to find waving tails in larger animals, and since no one had predicted, let alone observed, a 360 degree rotating joint, the thoughts and conclusions of generations of scientists had been colored by conscious and subconscious assumptions. What had been accepted as true turned out to be false. But remember, what was found to be true had in fact always been true.

We have little trouble with the idea of either tentatively accepting or rejecting theories. What is troublesome to us is that reasoned challenges to theories scientists adopt as scientifically self-evident, are often viewed as a return to the irrationality that preceded science. As such they are rejected without consideration as unworthy intrusions into pure science, which will go away if ignored.[54]

Many scientists simply will not talk about anything that upsets their idea of reality, yet all theories do just that. When any theory is first proposed, it is by its very nature an extension of humankind's knowledge (whether such knowledge is illusory or not), and as such goes beyond the then accepted view of the world. So long as such extensions are orderly and slow there is no problem, but when they leap ahead into the future they become the immediate concern of scientists who wish to keep science pure. There is a strong presumption that something that has not been proven is somehow less than true. To many people the unproved is not simply unproven, but is fantastic and worthy only of the title science fiction.

---

[53] Yeshitila Gebremichael, Gary S. Ayton, and Gregory A. Voth, "Mesoscopic Modeling of Bacterial Flagellar Microhydrodynamics," *Biophysics Journal* 91 (10) (November 2006): 3640–52. doi:10.1529/biophysj.106.091314
[54] Bernard Barber, "Resistance by Scientists to Scientific Discovery," *Science* 134 (1961): 596-602.
http://web.missouri.edu/~hanuscind/8710/Barber1961.pdf

Thus despite professed neutrality on that which has not been confirmed or rejected by experiment, many scientists have made it clear they are ready to label as absurd that which is significantly outside common experience and which has not been subjected to empirical scrutiny. If popular theories do not withstand future scientific challenges, recognition of their weakness will be slow to come, and acceptance of more exotic alternatives will be resisted with cries that the alternate theories are irrational myths. One should feel uneasy that correct theories, which are not subject to easy testing, might be dismissed as absurd. If something is currently "unproved" it may well be rejected by scientists as an impossibility, no one beyond the person postulating the theorem may dare dream of its truth.

As we have already noted, in addition to rejecting that which may be proven in the future, many scientists are equally willing to reject as an impossibility the existence of that which is beyond human perception, and thus "unprovable". No matter what we may think, or intuitively feel, we absolutely cannot reach any objective conclusions about that which is beyond human ability to prove or disprove. We can say nothing objective at all about the unprovable. The as of yet unproved, as well as the unprovable, may, or may not, be true.

We should note one type of statement, the definition, which can be viewed as an irrefutable truth.[55] By definition water "boils" at 100 degrees Celsius. You can always define something to be what you want it to be, yet no matter how you define an event you will not alter the physical reality that makes up the event. Water boils at 100 degrees because we have defined what water does at that temperature to be boiling. The word boiling is nothing more than a word chosen to describe what happens at a given temperature. As a definition it is a label, which has nothing to say about the physical laws that affect the water.

While we are as certain as we can be that water will continue to boil at 100 degrees, there can be no absolute guarantee that water will continue to act like it does when it gets

---

[55] Nuel Belnap,"On Rigorous Definitions," *Philosophical Studies* 72 no. 2 (1993): 115-146. http://www.jstor.org/stable/4320448

to 100 degrees. If in the future the behavior of water changes, scientists must either continue to label the new activity as boiling by broadening the meaning of the word, or must coin a new word to describe the changed state. If water would solidify instead of vaporizing, scientists could continue to define the new behavior as boiling and no one could say they were wrong.

Yet the new state would be totally opposite to the old, only the name would remain the same. Fortunately most observers recognize a responsibility not to use language to define away challenges to their beliefs, therefore they create new words to label new events.[56] The thing to remember is that definitions do not explain or alter the underlying reality.

---

[56] John A. Paulos, "Bigger Plates, More Food - Or Is It the Other Way Around?" *Scientific American* 305 (2011). doi:10.1038/scientificamerican1111-20

Reality Is Unreal

We know science cannot tell us anything about the world beyond our perception. What then can it tell us about the reality that surrounds us? Is it able to give us a sturdy foundation on which to build our lives? Can it answer our daily questions?

We will explore a bit of modern physics to see just how stable, or unstable, science really is. The information in this chapter is based on generally accepted theories at the time of writing, please note that by the time you read this book these theories may have been replaced by equally exotic scientific descriptions of reality. No matter what millennium you live in, you will be able to discover and recognize the absolute limits of science.

If we are to accept our observations of falling apples as proof of the law of gravity we must first assume several things, for instance, that our eyes accurately perceive the motion of the apple, that our ruler accurately measures the distance the apple travels, and that our watch correctly records the time it takes for it to drop. If confronted with the question "does the ruler you are using shrink and grow if you look at it while moving at different speeds?" most of us would laugh and say to ourselves of course it doesn't, a fixed length is what makes a ruler a ruler. We would think the person asking the question would have us questioning whether the apple is real.

Indeed we would have you question all scientific facts, for a scientist named Einstein shook the assumptions about distance, time, and space that scientists had relied on for thousands of years. In his theory of relativity he proved the length measured on a "perfect" ruler and the time measured on a "perfect" clock vary according to the relative motion of one object to another. Because the change in length and time is unbelievably small where relative speeds are slow, as in the case of a falling apple observed by an earthbound viewer, we can ignore the effect of relativity on everyday life.

None-the-less the effects are real and sensitive instruments have confirmed them. Because our eyes cannot measure any change in length does not mean that it is not occurring. The effect on a ruler becomes so great when relative speeds approach the speed of light that what was measured to be a foot actually becomes a millionth of a millionth of a millionth of an inch.[57]

Time is also affected by relative motion. If an identical twin could travel to another planet and back in a spaceship that flies at speeds approaching the speed of light, on return to Earth the space traveler would find that they had aged much less than their earthbound sibling.[58] Perhaps the astronaut would be only thirty years old while the earthbound twin would be ninety! This is not science fiction, the radical results predicted by relativity have been confirmed by countless experiments, including experiments where atomic clocks placed in jet planes ran slower than their earthbound counterparts!

Here is another example of an everyday fact taken for granted as being absolutely true. What is the shortest distance between two points? Without hesitation the answer for many, many years was a straight line. The theory of relativity tells us the universe may be shaped like a piecrust with bumps and valleys. Thus the shortest distance between any two points in the universe, whether it is between towns on earth or stars in space, must be drawn on the surface of the lumpy crust (the area outside the crust is outside the universe and does not exist) and, therefore, must be slightly curved![59]

Over the last few decades, some of the things which have been discovered are that energy and matter are different forms of the same thing ($e=mc^2$, energy = mass times the speed of light squared); the speed of light is constant and nothing can go faster than that speed; as matter approaches the speed of light it becomes infinitely massive and shrinks in its direction of motion

---

[57] D. V. Redžić, "Relativistic Length Agony Continued," *Serbian Astronomical Journal* 188 (2014): 55-65. doi:10.2298/SAJ1488055R

[58] Ronald C. Lasky, "Time and the Twin Paradox," *Scientific American* 23 (2014): 30-33. doi:10.1038/scientificamericantime1114-30

[59] Donna Roberts, "Euclidean and Non-Euclidean Geometry," *Regents Exam Prep Center* (2012).
http://www.regentsprep.org/regents/math/geometry/gg1/Euclidean.htm

to become infinitely small; at the sub-atomic level matter is neither a particle nor a wave but is incomprehensibly both; etc. There are several excellent books written for non-scientists that explain relativity and other topics in modern physics.[60]

Another foundation of modern science, quantum physics, appears to offer a description of reality that is radically different from the one relativity gives us. Rather than giving a single observable solution to a problem, laws that operate at the subatomic "quantum" level provide probabilities of observing one of many possible results. Quantum mechanics is a relatively new branch of science developed to explain why subatomic particles do not behave according to the Newtonian and relativistic laws that describe the behavior of normal size objects. Just prior to the time subatomic particles and events were first measured, physicists had declared that, with very minor exceptions, all the fundamental forces and laws of the universe had been discovered and described.

When scientists started to apply the traditional laws of physics to nuclear reactions they were literally amazed to find that the laws did not work! The search was on for a way to modify Newton's and Einstein's laws to explain the new phenomena. At the time no one knew the explanations would shake the very foundations of western knowledge.

Light is made up of energy in the form of photons which have mass (in motion) and which behave like particles, some of the time. The rest of the time photons behave like waves of energy, similar to ocean waves.[61] If you will think about an ocean

---

[60] Robert Geroch, *General Relativity from A to B*, (Chicago: University of Chicago Press, 1981); Paul Halpern, *Einstein's Dice and Schrodinger's Cat: How Two Great Minds Battled Quantum Randomness to Create a Unified Theory of Physics* (New York: Basic Books, 2015); Leonard Susskind and Art Friedman. *Quantum Mechanics: The Theoretical Minimum* (New York: Basic Books, 2014); Gary Zukav, *The Dancing Wu Li Masters: An Overview of the New Physics*. First printing 2001. (New York: Random House, 2012). [A bit dated but still easy reading.]
[61] Chad Orzel, "Particles and Waves: The Central Mystery of Quantum Mechanics?" YouTube Video, (2014): https://youtu.be/Hk3fgjHNQ2Q

wave you will realize water making up the wave simply moves up and down, not forward. Only the wave itself moves forward.

Thus if a boat is sitting a mile from shore, each wave will cause it to rise and fall, but will do little to move it toward shore. The boat will move a bit as each successive wave exerts a slight pushing force in the direction of the shore, but the boat won't be carried to shore by any one wave as the wave itself sweeps toward land. The vast majority of the water is simply moving up and down, while only the wave moves forward.[62]

The problem occurs when you try to measure photons using different tests. Some tests detect "particles" of light hitting targets while other tests detect "wave" interference when light passes through narrow slits. Back to the ocean example, when two ocean waves meet they either cancel each other if the trough of one overlaps the crest of the other, OR they reinforce each other when the crest of one joins the crest of the other, forming a single doubly big wave (any combination in-between can occur). When two waves interact they are said to be interfering with each other.[63]

---

[62] GCSE Science Revision, "Types of Waves," (2005). YouTube video. https://youtu.be/w2s2fZr8sqQ

[63] We hesitate to recommend clips from the movie "What the Bleep Do We Know" because the movie was produced by a Scientology like new age "cult" and had universally bad reviews "Some movies are so bad, they're funny. 'What the Bleep Do We Know,' a pseudoscientific docudrama that purports to link quantum mechanics and consciousness, would be a riot if people didn't take it so seriously.... What's most odious about 'What the Bleep,' though, is its message of profound self-absorption: The universe is all about you, and everything in your life is a product of your mind." – However this clip from the movie is the best we have seen on the two slit experiment, even though the part about observation is slightly misleading - Dr Quantum - Double Slit Experiment https://vimeo.com/109295025 Another clip, Dr Quantum - Flatland https://vimeo.com/108835396 is also a good explanation of dimensions. The full movie "Down the Rabbit Hole" has too many unsupported new age claims, and should only be watched by discerning new age skeptics with solid science backgrounds who want to waste some time.

The problem is a particle CANNOT act like a wave and a wave CANNOT act like a particle, yet photons act like both! The most popular solution of modern physics to this apparently unsolvable problem is to say that photons are neither waves nor particles until they are measured, and that the measurement itself determines the nature of the photon. In other words, it is the measurement of the event that determines the nature of the event.

To some degree this phenomena can be said to express hidden problems with what reality really is. In a sense physics is not able to describe the reality of an individual photon since it appears to have two inconsistent, coexistent, yet separate, natures. To the extent the point at which a photon is measured (known as the collapse of the wavefunction) can be considered an "event", an unsolved dilemma occurs in determining when the event "actualizes". If light is both a wave and a particle until measured,[64] is it truly a wave (when measured as a wave by an interference experiment) at the point it interferes with itself, or at the point it strikes a photographic plate, or at the time the film is developed, or at the point a human observes the final picture, etc.? The answer is simply not known.

One of the greatest scientific shocks came in the form of the Heisenberg uncertainty principal. To help explain the observed phenomena, Heisenberg noted that if you measure the momentum of one of the particles (momentum = velocity, which is speed in a given direction, times mass) that make up an atom you must in some way affect its position in an undeterminable way. For example, if you measure the momentum (or velocity, the uncertainty principal is equally true for both) of a subatomic particle by "observing" it move over a given distance, the

---

[64] Scientific American has a good short video on wave function collapse, however the conclusion that either the wave function does not exist or there are parallel universes is too simplistic and goes beyond the current state of theory – we really don't know the answer – take a look at this Scientific American Video, "What Is the Wave Function?" - https://youtu.be/aowYf44gDRY
See Mauro Dorato, "Events and the Ontology of Quantum Mechanics", *Topoi*, online, (March 2015). doi:10.1007/s11245-015-9315-6

observation alters its position in some unpredictable manner. Similarly, if you measure position you must alter momentum, thus at any given moment you CAN NEVER measure both the exact momentum and exact position of a subatomic particle.

The more precise you are in measuring momentum, the less precise you will be about position, and vice versa. The problem is actually more than a problem of measurement, to be more accurate, the wave function of a subatomic particle (which describes the particle at the quantum level) that has not been observed is precisely determined (without using probabilities) by a formula known as Schrodinger's wave equation.[65] However, the very moment you attempt to measure the momentum or position of the particle, the wave function collapses, introducing probabilities into the equation, and the exact momentum and position of the particle CANNOT be determined.

Heisenberg's theory can be interpreted as supporting the proposition that at the quantum level the very concepts of momentum and position have no real meaning. At the level of measured observation, modern physics can tell you how many particles in a group of particles have certain momentums and positions, and how many have other momentums and positions, but physicists CANNOT tell you what the momentum and position of any one particle is. This failure is far more than just some inability to measure momentum and position, it is due to the fact that it is fundamentally uncertain what the momentum and position of any single observed particle is! [66] A single particle when measured simply does not have position and momentum in

---

[65] Angelo Bassi, Kinjalk Lochan, Seema Satin, Tejinder P. Singh, and Hendrik Ulbricht. "Models of Wave-Function Collapse, Underlying Theories, and Experimental Tests," *Reviews of Modern Physics* 85 no. 2 (2013): 471. doi:10.1103/RevModPhys.85.471; Roger Penrose, "On the Gravitization of Quantum Mechanics 1: Quantum State Reduction," *Foundations of Physics* 44 no. 5 (2014): 557-575. doi:10.1007/s10701-013-9770-0
[66] Chad Orzel, "What is the Heisenberg Uncertainty Principle?" YouTube Video, (2014): https://youtu.be/TQKELOE9eY4

any normal sense of the words,[67] but members of a group do, and the probability of x number having x momentum and x,y,z position can be precisely computed!

One interpretation (there are others) of this finding is that nature appears to determine the behavior of its particles by a flip of a coin. Einstein spent the latter part of his life attempting to disprove this disturbing idea, it flew against his concept of the universe and prompted him to say, "God doesn't play dice with the world".[68] Yet he was unable to disprove quantum theory in general, and the included uncertainty principal in particular, both of which have correctly predicted every subatomic event that they have been tested against!

To emphasize the significance of the uncertainty principal remember it says that the uncertainty about momentum and position is not due to limitations on humankind's ability to make measurements, but rather is based on the apparent fact that when observed the momentum and position of an individual particle is fundamentally uncertain. Of course, future physicists may find an underlying set of rules that can be used to predict the behavior of individual particles, or may discover a fundamental unified law which is consistent with the observed behavior (an atemporal model may be found that works). Einstein's discomfort may well have been the result of human limitations on his understanding of God. Even though many questions remain unanswered, repudiation of the uncertainty principal, however comforting it would be to philosophers, seems uncertain at best.

One current theory, that is popular among cosmologists and that would eliminate the uncertainty, shows just how confusing and exotic the universe may be. The truly wild (and from some scientists' points of view virtually unbelievable)

---

[67] Gerd Leuchs, "The Physical Reality of the Quantum Wave Function," *arXiv preprint* (2014).
http://arxiv.org/ftp/arxiv/papers/1501/1501.07199.pdf
[68] William Hermanns, *Einstein and the Poet: In Search of the Cosmic Man,* (Wellesley, MA: Branden, 1983), 58.

many-worlds theory (multiverse)[69] suggests that every time an event occurs which has a possible required alternative, the universe splits into two identical parts, except that in one universe one alternative occurs, while in the other the other alternative occurs.[70] According to this theory (or at least to the most popular interpretations of it), there are potentially an infinite number of identical, except for the required alternatives, versions of each of us living simultaneously in different worlds. Uncertainty is eliminated because every alternative is guaranteed to occur. Rather than being a model of reality, this idea may be a product of human limitations.

If you want some more disturbing news we can give it to you. There is a controversial extension of quantum physics that deals with the problem of locality. Components of atoms have a property called spin. Spin is one of the fundamental quantities in the universe that must, and we do mean must, be conserved. For each particle that possesses positive spin, there MUST exist a particle with negative spin. When two entangled particles fly off in different directions from an atom, they always have opposite spin.

So far, no problems. We can change the spin of one of the entangled particles. The very instant we do so the other particle's spin changes, no matter what the distance is that separates them! Physicists, most of whom accept that a problem exists, are at a loss to explain how a particle in a different location without any means of communication knows what another particle's spin is. It is a mystery how one particle knows to change spin at the very instant the spin of the other particle is altered.[71] Recent

[69] Brian Greene, Ted Talk, "Why is Our Universe Fine-Tuned for Life?" https://youtu.be/bf7BXwVeyWw; Raphael Bousso and Leonard Susskind. "Multiverse Interpretation of Quantum Mechanics," *Physical Review D* 85 no. 4 (2012): 045007. doi:10.1103/PhysRevD.85.045007
[70] David Wallace, *The Emergent Multiverse: Quantum Theory According to the Everett Interpretation* (Oxford: Oxford University Press, 2012). [Best book on many-worlds theory.]
[71] Eric Powell, "Discover Interview: Anton Zeilinger Dangled From Windows, Teleported Photons, and Taught the Dalai Lama." *Discover Magazine* (August 2011). http://discovermagazine.com/2011/jul-aug/14-anton-zeilinger-teleports-photons-taught-the-dalai-lama

experiments seem to confirm this phenomena of "spooky" action at a distance.[72]

Einstein believed that any "rational", in the sense of "objective", description of nature is incomplete unless it is both a local and realistic theory. A theory is realistic if a particle has intrinsic properties that exist even before they are measured. A theory is local if measuring the properties of one particle cannot affect the properties of another, physically separated particle, in a length of time that would require communication between the particles that is faster than the speed of light. Yet quantum entanglement of spatially separated particles appears to require that realism, or locality, or both, be violated!

One explanation of entanglement eliminates the normal assumption of locality,[73] the assumption that events occur at one specific location in the space-time continuum.[74] If it is possible to have a rational description of the universe without a local theory,[75] then you can have events that appear to be occurring in different locations actually occurring in the same place.[76] Thus, no matter how far apart they may seem to be, two particles could know each other's spin because they are, in some as yet

---

[72] Chad Orzel, "Einstein's Brilliant Mistake: Entangled States," YouTube video. (2014). https://youtu.be/DbbWx2COU0E

[73] Edwin Eugene Klingman, *The Nature of Bell's Hidden Constraints* (2014). http://fqxi.org/data/essay-contest-files/Klingman_The_Nature_of_Bell.pdf While non-locality and entanglement seem real, questions still exist.

[74] Tim Maudlin, *Quantum Non-Locality and Relativity: Metaphysical Intimations of Modern Physics* (Hoboken: John Wiley and Sons, 2011).

[75] Nicolas Brunner, Daniel Cavalcanti, Stefano Pironio, Valerio Scarani, and Stephanie Wehner. "Bell Nonlocality," *Reviews of Modern Physics* 86 no. 2 (2014): 419. doi:10.1103/RevModPhys.86.419; Roman V. Buniy, and Stephen DH Hsu. "Everything Is Entangled," *Physics Letters B* 718 no. 2 (2012): 233-236. doi:10.1016/j.physletb.2012.09.047

[76] Paul S. Wesson, "The Status of Modern Five-Dimensional Gravity," arXiv preprint (2014). http://arxiv.org/ftp/arxiv/papers/1412/1412.6136.pdf

unexplained manner, in the same location.[77] Perhaps the two particles occupy the same position in some unknown dimension where there is no such thing as separation. Speculation about the significance of lack of locality is really unproductive,[78] except to note that lack of locality could help explain premonitions and extrasensory events.[79]

Other complex examples of conflicts with accepted concepts of reality, truth, and classical philosophy and logic, are found within the fascinating, unsettling, discoveries of modern physics. We are left with fundamental paradoxes, the solutions to which are totally unknown. Indeed, despite what we are told by many scientists, it is not at all clear to those working at the leading edge of scientific inquiry that an objective physical description of the universe actually exists.

The destruction of traditional concepts of time, space, matter, energy, of life itself, is both frightening, and hopeful. Given the dramatic efforts of modern physics to unravel the mysteries

---

[77] Again, we hesitate to recommend clips from the movie "What the Bleep Do We Know" because the movie was produced by a Scientology like new age "cult" and had universally bad reviews, however this clip on quantum entanglement from the movie is a concise 1.5 minute summary of entanglement (it may be an overstatement that everything is touching) https://vimeo.com/108956253 As we noted before, the full movie "Down the Rabbit Hole" has too many unsupported new age claims, and should only be watched by discerning new age skeptics with solid science backgrounds who want to waste some time.

[78] Research on nonlocality and entanglement is in the early stages - Giuseppe Vallone, Gustavo Lima, Esteban S. Gómez, Gustavo Canas, Jan-Åke Larsson, Paolo Mataloni, and Adán Cabello. "Bell Scenarios in Which Nonlocality and Entanglement Are Inversely Related," *Physical Review A* 89 no. 1 (2014). doi:10.1103/PhysRevA.89.012102; J. Tura, A. B. Sainz, T. Grass, R. Augusiak, A. Acín, and M. Lewenstein. "Entanglement and Nonlocality in Many-Body Systems: A Primer," *arXiv preprint* (2015). http://arxiv.org/pdf/1501.02733.pdf

[79] Harald Walach, Walter von Lucadou, and Hartmann Römer, "Parapsychological Phenomena as Examples of Generalized Nonlocal Correlations-A Theoretical Framework." *Journal of Scientific Exploration* 28 no. 4 (2014): 605-631.

of the physical world, coupled with the possibility of the discovery of theories that better explain space-time (or atemporal space), perhaps even the discovery and/or existence of other dimensions, all manner of extraordinary event may eventually be explained.[80] Yet it is also possible that, despite appearances to the contrary, the universe does not have an objective and/or observable fundamental physical nature, and that no explanation is possible.

Again we need to remember that all theories owe their credibility to repeated statistical successes. Even in the case of generally accepted physical laws, like the ones we have just discussed, one observed deviation would result in the probability of the theorem being correct going to zero. When a theory is for the first time shown to be false it is not merely more likely to be false, IT IS FALSE. On the other hand, the more observations reported which confirm the predictions of a law, the higher the probability is that the law is true. No matter how many observations are made, the possibility will always exist that the law is in fact false. The bottom line is that we cannot prove or disprove anything with absolute certainty, and we cannot say anything objective at all about that which we cannot observe.

---

[80] Von Baeyer, Hans Christian. "Quantum Weirdness? It's All In Your Mind," *Scientific American* 308 no. 6 (2013): 46-51. doi:10.1038/scientificamerican0613-46 We believe that quantum information theory is too simple a solution.

Cosmology

A passing glance at cosmology, where science faces the problem of nothing, may be useful to our later discussions. Until recently it was assumed that science could not reach back before the creation of our universe, the so called big bang.[81] In 1977 astronomer Virginia Trimble echoed the sentiment of most cosmologists, "Unfortunately, this hot, dense phase (sometimes called the Big Bang) also wiped out any evidence of what (if anything) went before. Hence the question what happened before the Big Bang belongs to the realm of pure speculation (philosophy?) rather than that of physics."[82] Yet even then the idea was being explored that quantum physics had something to do with the early universe.[83] "The great advances made in physical cosmology over the past few years open a window for the consideration of issues long dismissed as philosophical speculations."[84]

In recent years[85] there has been an effort to reconcile the general relativity of Einstein with Quantum field theory, through

---

[81] Martin Bojowald, "What Happened Before the Big Bang?" *Nature Physics* 3 (2007): 523-525. doi:10.1038/nphys654

[82] Virginia Trimble, "Cosmology: Man's Place in the Universe: In Which We Review the History of the Universe and Explore the Relationships between Its Properties and the Presence of Life," *American Scientist* (1977): 76-86.
http://www.jstor.org/discover/10.2307/27847645

[83] Robert Brout, François Englert, and Edgard Gunzig. "The Creation of the Universe as a Quantum Phenomenon," *Annals of Physics* 115 (1978): 78-106. doi: 10.1016/0003-4916(78)90176-8

[84] Susana J. Landau, Claudia G. Scóccola, and Daniel Sudarsky, "Cosmological Constraints on Nonstandard Inflationary Quantum Collapse Models," *Physical Review D* 85 no. 12 (2012): 123001. doi:10.1103/PhysRevD.85.123001

[85] Actually these ideas have been floating around for quite some time - Edward Grant, ed. *Much Ado about Nothing: Theories of Space and Vacuum from the Middle Ages to the Scientific Revolution* (Cambridge: Cambridge University Press, 1981); Peter W. Milonni and Claudia Eberlein, "The Quantum Vacuum: An Introduction to Quantum Electrodynamics," *American Journal of Physics* 62 no. 12 (1994): 1154-1154.

a theory of quantum gravity.[86] This has led to the idea that before there was any matter,[87] before the first anything, there was a quantum fluctuation that created the very first something out of *nothing*.[88] The reason that this might even be possible is that in quantum field theory a particle does not exist until it is observed, only the probability that a particle will be found exists. Since the probability is not a particle, it is proposed that the probability is essentially *nothing*. When the first probability actualized and a particle was formed, that particle would arguably have come out of *nothing*.[89]

While the idea of something out of *nothing* is attractive since it suggests a mechanism for creation before the big bang, it has many problems.[90] First, and most important, scientists do not understand quantum physics. They certainly have developed a strong base in quantum field theory but they simply do not understand quantum gravity or quantum cosmology. Until we have a better theory we cannot know if the quantum vacuum is truly empty like the classical vacuum, and we should not assume

---

[86] Abhay Ashtekar, Martin Reuter, and Carlo Rovelli, "From General Relativity to Quantum Gravity," arXiv preprint (2014): http://fr.arxiv.org/pdf/1408.4336; Callender, *Physics Meets Philosophy at the Planck Scale: Contemporary Theories in Quantum Gravity*; Mauro Dorato, "Rovelli's Relational Quantum Mechanics, Anti-Monism and Quantum Becoming." arXiv preprint (2013): http://arxiv.org/ftp/arxiv/papers/1309/1309.0132.pdf

[87] G. S. Paraoanu, "The Quantum Vacuum" arXiv preprint (2014): http://arxiv.org/pdf/1402.1087.pdf

[88] Krauss, *a Universe from Nothing*.

[89] Dongshan He, Dongfeng Gao, and Qing-yu Cai. "Spontaneous Creation of the Universe from Nothing," *Physical Review D* 89 (2014): 083510. doi:10.1103/PhysRevD.89.083510

[90] Glenn B. Siniscalchi, "A Response to Professor Krauss on Nothing," Heythrop Journal 54 (2013): 678-690. doi :10.1111/heyj.12018 - Written from a theological perspective, this article identifies both philosophical and theologic challenges to the theory; Claus Kiefer, "Conceptual Problems in Quantum Gravity and Quantum Cosmology," *ISRN Mathematical Physics* (2013). doi: 10.1155/2013/509316

that particles created from quantum fluctuations actually come from *nothing*.[91]

"Although quantum mechanics (QM) and quantum field theory (QFT) are highly successful, the seemingly simplest state - vacuum - remains mysterious."[92] We know that we can "shake" photons out of the vacuum,[93] but the idea that we are creating a particle out of *nothing* may be misleading. It seems likely that matter, including dark matter, is more closely tied to vacuum energy states than we realize (e = mc²).[94] It may be that matter was not created from *nothing*, rather there may have been a more complex quantum energy fluctuation than we currently imagine. Our intuition is that something called loop quantum gravity theory is the most promising inquiry, and that we will eventually find that the quantum vacuum is populated by force / energy / matter that at present is either not known or not understood. If we look far enough before the big bang we may or may not find *nothing*.

What about the end of the universe? John Baez, a physicist who has excellent communications skills, says about the end of the universe: "But the overall picture seems to lean heavily towards a far future [billions of years from now] where everything consists of isolated stable particles: electrons, neutrinos, and protons (unless protons decay). If the scenario I'm describing is correct, the density of these particles will go to zero, and eventually each one will be cut off from all the rest by a cosmological horizon, making them unable to interact. Of course there will be photons as well, but these will eventually come into thermal equilibrium forming blackbody radiation at the

---

[91] Charles Choi, "Something from Nothing? A Vacuum Can Yield Flashes of Light," *Scientific American* (February 2013). http://www.scientificamerican.com/article/something-from-nothing-vacuum-can-yield-flashes-of-light

[92] E. Milotti, F. Della Valle, G. Zavattini, G. Messineo, U. Gastaldi, R. Pengo, G. Ruoso et al. "Exploring Quantum Vacuum with Low-Energy Photons," *International Journal of Quantum Information* 10 (2012). doi: 10.1142/S021974991241002X

[93] Diego Dalvit, "Quantum Physics: Shaking Photons Out of the Vacuum," *Nature* 479 (2011): 303-304. doi:10.1038/479303a

[94] Ibid.

temperature of the cosmological horizon - perhaps about 10^{-30} Kelvin or so."[95] So at the end the universe may be made up of what philosophers call simples, indivisible particles, totally isolated from each other.

All this leads us to the question of consciousness, is it a physical phenomena or is it, at least partially, non-physical and beyond human observation? Does human consciousness end, or does it continue, after physical death. Can it survive the end of the physical universe? Because we cannot prove, or disprove, that we continue to exist after the death of our bodies does not mean that our consciousness does not continue to exist, or that it does. If we continue to exist after our physical death, then we continue to exist, and if we do not, then we do not.

---

[95] John Baez, "The End of the Universe" (2011): From
http://math.ucr.edu/home/baez/end.html

Consciousness

Now that we have a basic understanding of science, we will apply the scientific method to the phenomena of consciousness. In the third millennium we would think that science has an answer to the question what does it mean to be conscious, however consciousness is one of the greatest mysteries of our existence.

Scientists may tell us that our choices are mechanical selections based on some complex biological decision making scheme. They might point to the similarity between computers and the brain's neural networks as proof of a purely evolutionary process behind consciousness. Yet most would admit that we really don't understand how consciousness can arise out of neurologic activity alone. It is fair to conclude that most scientists do not believe we have found a satisfactory explanation of, or mechanism for, human consciousness.

For our purposes the most popular theories about consciousness can be summarized and grouped (we borrow from Stuart Hameroff's classifications)[96] as follows:

(1) Physical Consciousness – Dependent. Consciousness is something that is the product of and dependent on our physical bodies, it does not exist outside the individual physical brain. The argument is that consciousness evolved naturally through complex biological adaptation of brains and nervous systems into the computational prodigy of human thought.[97] The mind and brain are the same,[98] consciousness is the product of physical,

---

[96] Stuart Hameroff, *Quantum Consciousness* (2015).
http://www.quantumconsciousness.org/
[97] Jaan Aru, Talis Bachmann, Wolf Singer, and Lucia Melloni, "Distilling the Neural Correlates of Consciousness," *Neuroscience and Biobehavioral Reviews* 36 no. 2 (2012): 737-746. doi:10.1016/j.neubiorev.2011.12.003
[98] Michael A. Cohen and Daniel C. Dennett, "Consciousness Cannot be Separated from Function," *Trends in Cognitive Sciences* 15 no. 8 (2011): 358-364. doi:10.1016/j.tics.2011.06.008

neurological, processes in the brain and nervous system.[99] This may be the most widely accepted view of scientists and modern philosophers. Opinions vary as to when, where, and how consciousness appeared, e.g. only recently in humans or earlier in lower organisms,[100] but those who espouse this view agree that human consciousness begins at physical birth and ends at physical death.

Conscious beings have an advantage in the survival of the fittest. As an evolutionary adaptation physical consciousness produced by the brain is commonly assumed to be epiphenomenal (i.e. an effect without independent agency), and also illusory (largely constructing rather than perceiving reality). In this view, consciousness is not an independent, fundamental, quality of existence, but rather a phenomena so complex that human beings have not identified the underlying mechanism.[101]

(2) Physical / Natural Consciousness[102] – Independent. Consciousness is something that exists outside the physical, it is not dependent on the physical brain, but it is still governed by the physical and natural laws of the universe. Natural laws are those laws of nature which control everything not subject to what scientists call physical laws. In the future natural laws may be

---

[99] Simon van Gaal and Victor AF Lamme, "Unconscious High-Level Information Processing Implication for Neurobiological Theories of Consciousness," *The Neuroscientist* 18 no. 3 (2012): 287-301. doi: 10.1177/1073858411404079

[100] Michael C. Corballis, *The Recursive Mind: The Origins of Human Language, Thought, and Civilization* (Princeton: Princeton University Press, 2014).

[101] D. Dennett, *Consciousness Explained* (Boston: Little, Brown and Company, 1991); Talis Bachmann and Anthony G. Hudetz, "It is Time to Combine the Two Main Traditions in the Research on the Neural Correlates of Consciousness: C= L× D," *Consciousness Research* 5 (2014): 940. doi:10.3389/fpsyg.2014.00940

[102] When we use the term "physical / natural consciousness", or "natural consciousness" associated with physical consciousness, we are referring to consciousness constrained by and dependent on the physical and natural laws of the universe, we are not referring to "non-physical consciousness" which is independent of and not constrained by those laws.

found to be part of a unified set of physical laws, but at least for now the connection is not obvious. Consciousness is something more than the physical brain, it is an independent, fundamental, quality of existence, which is necessary to explain the experience of perception[103] and qualia.[104] None-the-less it is the product of physical laws and/or natural laws which are not yet, and which may never be, understood.[105]

The mind and brain are two separate entities, with the mind acting through the agency of the brain. Qualia are the subjective properties of experiences, what it feels like to see a red sunset over the ocean. Qualia are the phenomenal properties of human experiences, they are a product of the mind, which is part of the natural physical world. "The world still consists in a network of fundamental properties related by basic laws, and everything is to be ultimately explained in those terms. All that has happened is that the inventory of properties and laws has been expanded [beyond what is now known as the physical]."[106]

There are different ideas about natural laws.[107] Many view natural laws as deterministic rules that were set in place at the beginning of the universe and that control those events which are not subject to physical laws. This group includes those Deists[108] who believe that God created the universe and without further

---

[103] Ned Block, "Perceptual Consciousness Overflows Cognitive Access," *Trends in Cognitive Sciences* 15 no. 12 (2011): 567-575. doi:10.1016/j.tics.2011.11.001; Alva Noë and Evan Thompson, eds. *Vision and Mind: Selected Readings in the Philosophy of Perception.* (Cambridge: MIT Press, 2002).

[104] Frank Jackson, "Epiphenomenal Qualia," *The Philosophical Quarterly* (1982): 127-136. http://www.jstor.org/stable/2960077

[105] David Chalmers, *The Conscious Mind: In Search of a Fundamental Theory* (Oxford: Oxford University Press, 1996).

[106] Ibid., 127-8.

[107] Bernard Williams, *Descartes: The Project of Pure Enquiry,* (New York: Routledge, 2014).

[108] Byrne, P. *Natural Religion and the Nature of Religion: The Legacy of Deism* (London: Routledge, 2013). Deists may posit that there are only physical laws and be monist physicalists, or may recognize deterministic natural laws and be subject dualists.

intervention allows it to evolve according to the laws of nature. We include as proponents of the Physical / Natural Consciousness – Independent classification only those who believe that consciousness is part of the universe, constrained by the laws of physics and nature. Consciousness may be immaterial, yet it is a phenomena which is a fundamental part of, and dependent on, the existence of the universe.

The idea of mind as consciousness that is independent of the brain has become more interesting since we have experimentally verified quantum entanglement (at least tentatively). The possible significance of quantum entanglement (QE) is, as we briefly noted in the last chapter, that there may be an instantaneous, verifiable, connection between the brain and the mind, perhaps even a connection between conscious beings. If there is a connection between all conscious beings there may be some form of universal consciousness which we have no present understanding of. This is not a mystical possibility, rather if true it may be the consequence of all matter, including our brains, being a part of the "energy" of the universe (vastly oversimplified as $e = mc^2$).[109] Indeed, some suggest this lends support to the ancient idea of a universal natural consciousness encompassing all physical matter (panpsychism).[110]

A key concept in both our first and second classifications is that consciousness, whether located in the brain or mind or both, is a phenomena constrained by being a part of the fundamental properties of the world. The mind and brain may be the same thing, or the mind may be a different substance, it might

---

[109] Diederik Aerts, Liane Gabora, and Sandro Sozzo, "Concepts and Their Dynamics: A Quantum-Theoretic Modeling of Human Thought," *Topics in Cognitive Science* 5 no. 4 (2013): 737-772. doi: 10.1111/tops.12042

[110] C. Koch, "Is Consciousness Universal?" *Scientific American Mind* 25 (2014): 26-29. http://www.scientificamerican.com/article/is-consciousness-universal/; Giulio Tononi, "Integrated Information Theory of Consciousness: An Updated Account," *Archives Italiennes de Biologie* 150 (2012): 56-90. http://www.architalbiol.org/aib/article/viewFile/15056/23165867; John Searle, *The Mystery of Consciousness* (New York: New York Review of Books, 1997). Searle finds panpsychism to be absurd.

be independent. The mind may even exist for a finite period of time beyond the physical death of the brain, none-the-less physical / natural consciousness is a fundamental, not an independent, property of the universe.

We noted that cosmologic theories posit that the universe will eventually end or will reach a meaningless state of maximum entropy. Even if we live in a cyclical universe there will be periodic episodes of environments which appear to be hostile to the existence of any sentient being. Despite its independent nature, physical / natural consciousness would almost certainly not survive those periods.

You may see references to discontinuity theory and continuity theory. Discontinuity theorists favor our first classification (Physical Consciousness – Dependent). They believe that consciousness appeared at a later stage through random mutation that conferred a survival of the fittest advantage throughout the evolution of complex life. They see human consciousness as physical and dependent on the brain.

Continuity theorists usually favor our second classification (Physical / Natural Consciousness – Independent). They endorse a form of panpsychism consciousness which co-emerged with matter at the big bang and co-evolves with it.[111] As carbon-based life forms developed into creatures with sensory 'qualia', self-consciousness developed alongside evolutionary biologic changes. It is an independent consciousness that is separate from, yet is associated with and dependent on, matter.

While it has autonomous properties, the mind is still seen by continuity theorists as created by and part of a world that is both physical and natural. Consciousness may be continuous over a finite period, yet most continuity theorists would agree that at some point after physical death the self-aware consciousness associated with a physical human being ends. Sometime after the physical death of an individual a disembodied self-aware consciousness which can be said to be the person no longer exists.

---

[111] Max Velmans, *Understanding Consciousness* (London: Routledge, 2009).

It seems intuitively true that all consciousness based on physical laws, and if they exist natural laws, will cease to exist on or before periods which cannot sustain sentient life. We do not have scientific proof that this is true, indeed the idea of existential meaning presupposes some immaterial yet permanent form of individual sentient consciousness inherent in physical and natural laws. However there is no objective, or convincing subjective, evidence of immaterial consciousness that is not dependent on a physical universe capable of supporting biologic life. Even if there is universal sentience which is a fundamental part of the physical universe it would intuitively seem to be diffuse, something that would not preserve individual human consciousness. There is no reasonable interpretation of theories of physical and/or natural laws which would allow for permanent, individual, human consciousness.

(3) Non-Physical Consciousness - Independent. Consciousness is a fundamental quality of existence that is not controlled by physical and natural laws. Religious souls and other spirit understandings assume consciousness has an independent non-physical existence that is not dependent on "fundamental properties related by basic laws".[112] Consciousness might causally influence physical matter and human behavior, but it does not owe its existence to, is not a property of, and cannot be controlled by, physical or natural laws of the world. This allows for belief in a permanent consciousness that survives physical death and the end of the universe. Some describe this consciousness as a gift of God, a creative force, the essence of the universe. Consciousness that resides in the non-physical soul is outside scientific observation, so that science cannot say anything objective, either positive or negative, about it.

We will not prove or eliminate any of the three major classifications, however we will argue that the third, non-physical consciousness independent from the existence of properties of the world, is a rational, logical, possibility. We will also argue that of the three possibilities Non-Physical Consciousness - Independent is the only one capable of providing a rational

---

[112] Chalmers, *The Conscious Mind*, 127-8

reason for human existence. But first we need to understand the consequences of each of the models.

Human and Animal Consciousness

What is the significance of human consciousness? Intuitively, the choices we make in life seem to be based not only on what we believe will happen if we make a certain choice, but also on what we want to happen. We believe that we possess the ability to engage in what we will call "rational thought", whereby each of us weighs many variables in a process that includes concepts of good and evil, right and wrong. Rational thought, as we define it, is reasoned[113] thought which presents us with choices between alternatives. You feel, rightly or wrongly, that you ultimately reach a point in your rational thinking where that certain quality of conscious being which is unique to you takes over and you make your choice among the alternatives.

Biologists have demonstrated that the line between animal[114] and human rational thought is not as clear as was once commonly assumed.[115] An obvious challenge to the uniqueness of human thought is the fact that insects, even single cell amoeba, show signs of what some believe to be consciousness.[116] "It is puzzling that primitive organisms that lack any kind of nervous system show sophisticated behaviors that we assume require a nervous system with some sort of centralized brain or

---

[113] Hugo Mercier and Dan Sperber, "Why Do Humans Reason? Arguments for an Argumentative Theory," *Behavioral and Brain Sciences* 34 no. 02 (2011): 57-74. doi:10.1017/S0140525X10000968
[114] Gyula K. Gajdon, Melanie Lichtnegger, and Ludwig Huber, "What a Parrot's Mind Adds to Play: The Urge to Produce Novelty Fosters Tool Use Acquisition in Kea," *Open Journal of Animal Sciences* 4 no. 02 (2014): 51.doi:10.4236/ojas.2014.42008
[115] Stephen M. Downes, and Edouard Machery, *Arguing About Human Nature: Contemporary Debates* (New York: Routledge, 2013).
[116] Anthony J. Trewavas and František Baluška. "The Ubiquity of Consciousness," *EMBO Reports* 12 (2011): 1221-1225. doi:10.1038/embor.2011.218

ganglion."[117] In 1902 Harvard biologist Charles Minot[118] said, "A frank unbiased study of consciousness must convince every biologist that it is one of the fundamental phenomena of at least all animal life if not, as is quite possible, of all life teleological".[119]

There are animals which appear to have self-awareness, solve problems, communicate, exhibit emotions,[120] etc. While there may be a very high degree of intelligence in the animal world,[121] it seems that animals lack the ability to make choices by consciously engaging in "rational thought" about alternatives and consequences.[122] It appears that only human beings possess the necessary consciousness and symbolic languages that allow us to engage in significant abstract, rational, thought.[123]

---

[117] John Tyler Bonner, "Brainless Behavior: A Myxomycete Chooses a Balanced Diet," *Proceedings of the National Academy of Sciences* 107 no. 12 (2010): 5267-5268. doi:10.1073/pnas.1000861107; Hans V. Westerhoff, Aaron N. Brooks, Evangelos Simeonidis, Rodolfo García-Contreras, Fei He, Fred C. Boogerd, Victoria J. Jackson, Valeri Goncharuk, and Alexey Kolodkin, "Macromolecular Networks and Intelligence in Microorganisms," *Frontiers in Microbiology* 5 (2014). doi: 10.3389/fmicb.2014.00379

[118] Charles S. Minot, *Modern Problems of Biology* (Philadelphia: Blakiston, 1913).

[119] Charles S. Minot, "The Problem of Consciousness in Its Biological Aspects," *Science* 16 no. 392 (1902): 1-12. http://www.jstor.org/stable/1628678

[120] Frans De Waal, "What is an Animal Emotion?" *Annals of the New York Academy of Sciences* 1224 no. 1 (2011): 191-206. doi: 10.1111/j.1749-6632.2010.05912.x

[121] Esther Herrmann and Josep Call. "Are There Geniuses Among the Apes?" *Philosophical Transactions of the Royal Society B: Biological Sciences* 367 no. 1603 (2012): 2753-2761.doi:10.1098/rstb.2012.0191

[122] Joëlle Proust, "The Limits of Animal Thought Are Still Unknown," In *The Philosophy of Metacognition: Mental Agency and Self-awareness* (Oxford: Oxford University Press, 2013).

[123] Daniel Cloud, *The Domestication of Language: Cultural Evolution and the Uniqueness of the Human Animal* (West Sussex: Columbia University Press, 2014); Jonathan St Evans, "Dual-processing Accounts of Reasoning, Judgment, and Social Cognition," *Annual Revue*

For example, animals may or may not harm other animals, yet they do not appear to be able to make reasoned choices to harm or not to harm by considering whether it is right or wrong to do so.[124] An animal may make a choice to act kindly toward another animal[125] based in part on their inherent personality and basic instincts.[126] Yet it appears that an animal cannot make a rational, reasoned, choice[127] to go against inherent personality and basic instincts.[128]

Human beings can choose to do that which they would not otherwise do, to go against what their instincts, personality, and emotions tell them to do. We sometimes take this apparent distinction for granted. Rather than consider ourselves to be little more than highly evolved animals, we should recognize and give

---

Psychology 59 (2008): 255-278. doi: 10.1146/annurev.psych.59.103006.093629; Keith E. Stanovich, "On the Distinction Between Rationality and Intelligence: Implications for Understanding Individual Differences in Reasoning," In *The Oxford Handbook of Thinking and Reasoning* (Oxford: Oxford Press, 2012), 343-365.

[124] Robert W. Lurz, ed. *The Philosophy of Animal Minds* (Cambridge: Cambridge University Press, 2009).

[125] Frans de Waal, "The Antiquity of Empathy," *Science* 336, no. 6083 (2012): 874-876. doi: 10.1126/science.1222069

[126] Herbert L. Roitblat, H. S. Terrace, and T. G. Bever, eds. *Animal Cognition* (New York: Psychology Press, 2014).

[127] Jonathan St Evans, "Two Minds Rationality," *Thinking and Reasoning* 20 no. 2 (2014): 129-146. doi:10.1080/13546783.2013.845605

[128] An argument for animal morality is found in Frans de Waal, ed. *Evolved Morality: The Biology and Philosophy of Human Conscience* (Leiden: Brill, 2014). Evolutionary morality does not address the apparent inability of animals to invoke rational thought processes to act against what evolutionary morality dictates, we do not know of any evidence that animals possess the ability, as humans apparently do, to engage in free will rational thought which results in their acting against inherent personality and biologic instincts.

more consideration to what appears to be our unique ability to engage in "rational thought".[129]

Unlike any animal, our choices are made after rational thought.[130] This distinction does not deny that some animals choose to risk their own lives to protect other animals, rather it asserts that humans are able to engage in reasoned thought before making the choice to risk or not to risk their lives. Even though you have instinctive feelings for self-preservation, procreation, self-satisfaction, etc., decisions may be freely made for reasons and purposes totally opposite to those instincts.

You can think about what you are going to do, and can choose to do what you believe is right and good even if it places you in grave danger. Similarly, you can choose to do what you believe is wrong and evil even if you would instinctively do otherwise. Your decision is your decision, a product of your singular existence and being.[131] Able to engage in rational thought,[132] and to choose freely among various courses of action based on those thoughts, you are in a very real sense what you choose to be.

We may eventually find that the distinction between reasoned thought and autonomic animal behavior is not significant. However, we will proceed to the next challenge to being human with the assumption that human beings are

---

[129] John C. Avise and Francisco J. Ayala, "In the Light of Evolution IV: The Human Condition," *Proceedings of the National Academy of Sciences* 107 Supplement 2 (2010): 8897-8901. doi:10.1073/pnas.1003214107

[130] Francisco J. Ayala, "The Difference of Being Human: Morality," *Proceedings of the National Academy of Sciences* 107 Supplement 2 (2010): 9015-9022. doi :10.1073/pnas.0914616107; Peter Carruthers, "Animal Subjectivity," *Psyche* 4 no. 3 (1998): 1-7. http://journalpsyche.org/files/0xaa52.pdf

[131] Despite our intuitive feelings, the nature of human free will remains controversial, Robert Kane, ed. *The Oxford Handbook of Free Will* (Oxford: Oxford University Press, 2011).

[132] Maggie E. Toplak, Richard F. West, and Keith E. Stanovich, "Rational Thinking and Cognitive Sophistication: Development, Cognitive Abilities, and Thinking Dispositions," *Developmental Psychology* 50 no. 4 (2014): 1037. doi:10.1037/a0034910

conscious beings who make personal decisions based on uniquely rational thought.

Quantum Consciousness

We need to take a side trip to discuss the eminent mathematician, Roger Penrose's, thoughts on consciousness. In a series of books starting in 1994,[133] he suggests that free will is explained by the uncertainty principal of quantum theory. Microtubules are a component of the cytoskeleton of neurons in the brain and elsewhere, they are the filaments through which electrical activity flows from cell to cell.[134] For over twenty years Penrose, and his collaborator Stuart Hameroff, have suggested that quantum effects occur in the microtubules that can be influenced by the environment.[135] Their controversial theory Orchestrated Objective Reduction (OrchOR) languished until recent evidence[136] showed quantum vibrations in microtubules.[137]

---

[133] Roger Penrose, *The Road to Reality: A Complete Guide to the Laws of the Universe* (London: Jonathan Cape, 2014; Roger Penrose, *The Emperor's New Mind: Concerning Computers, Minds, and the Laws of Physics* (Oxford: Oxford University Press, 1999); Roger Penrose, *Shadows of the Mind* (Oxford: Oxford University Press, 1994).

[134] See Jill U. Adams, "Cytoskeletal Networks Provide Spatial Organization and Mechanical Support to Eukaryotic Cells," In ed. Clare O'Connor *Essentials of Cell Biology* (New York: Nature Publishing Group, 2014); P. W. Baas and F. J. Ahmad, "Beyond Taxol: Microtubule-Based Treatment of Disease and Injury of the Nervous System," *Brain* 136 no. 10 (2013): 2937-2951. doi:10.1093/brain/awt153

[135] Stuart Hameroff and Roger Penrose, "Consciousness in the Universe: A Review of the 'Orch OR' Theory," *Physics of Life Reviews* 11 no. 1 (2014): 39-78. doi:10.1016/j.plrev.2013.08.002

[136] A. Bandyopadhyay, *Study of Opto-electronic Properties of a Single Microtubule in the Microwave Regime* (Tsukuba Ibaraki: National Institute for Materials Science, 2013). http://www.dtic.mil/dtic/tr/fulltext/u2/a554174.pdf

[137] Satyajit Sahu, Subrata Ghosh, Kazuto Hirata, Daisuke Fujita, and Anirban Bandyopadhyay, "Multi-level Memory-Switching Properties of a Single Brain Microtubule," *Applied Physics Letters* 102 no. 12 (2013): 123701. doi:10.1063/1.4793995

Basically, Penrose believes that there is a quantum component in the transmission of neurologic impulses from one neuron to another which provides sufficient opportunity to influence the actualization of the quantum state (i.e. – to objectively alter the probabilities so that they are skewed toward one result). This is far more than a version of the Copenhagen interpretation of quantum mechanics, which says that observation collapses the quantum wave function, rather it suggests that selection of probabilities in neurons may be orchestrated in a flood of quantum interactions "controlled" by human thought. Recent acceptance of the existence of non-local quantum entanglement may strengthen his idea even more.

OrchOR is not by necessity (as some think) a non-physical theory, rather in its present form it is a physical explanation of how a massively cooperating set of neurons can select between multiple choices by subtly altering quantum probabilities, likely through the physical mechanism of QE. This may or may not be the source of free will consciousness, perhaps there is an even deeper layer of quantum effects in the brain / mind, or perhaps this line of inquiry will be a dead-end. Intuitively OrchOR and the underlying concepts seem to us to be the most promising avenue of inquiry into physical consciousness.

So does consciousness provide meaning in life? Is the difference between our pet rock and us the fact that we can observe our surroundings and our rock cannot? If that is the only difference, what happens when we experience physical death and join our pet rock as just another unconscious inanimate object? How do philosophers answer our questions?

Philosophy

It is time to introduce the other major players in the consciousness debate, philosophers. We have briefly mentioned a few of the philosophical parallels to scientific theories. We will revisit some of the issues we just uncovered using the scientific method. Philosophers share the same curiosity about consciousness and existence that scientists possess.[138] It would take many volumes to do justice to philosopher's arguments, but we will at least survey the landscape and see how philosophical approaches to solving our dilemmas might work.

The reason that we bring philosophers on stage now is because 1) we need to figure out if a physical and/or non-physical conscious existence is necessary for human life to have *meaning* and 2) if so, is it a necessary condition for *meaning* that conscious existence not end. We will look at existence and then come back to consciousness. If the philosophy chapters give you a headache don't feel bad, we are flying through ideas that take years to fully comprehend.

---

[138] Robert Klee, ed., *Scientific Inquiry* (New York: Oxford University Press, 1999).

Existence

At the start of this book we said we want to explore *nothing*. A great deal of the problem is trying to understand what we might mean by absolute *nothing*.[139] If we say that there are no unicorns does that mean that unicorns do not exist now, or that unicorns did not exist in the past, or that unicorns can never exist in the future?

What we will not do is take sides in the metaphysical and scientific debates. We will instead see if for our purposes a common sense approach suffices.[140] It is common sense that an object exists if a set of conditions is satisfied that causes the object to be observable.[141] It is simple to say that our pet rock exists because it is easily observed to be a solid object in the palm of our hand, but it is not so simple to declare that a unique living organism exists.[142]

Who is On First?

What does it mean to exist? The metaphysical study of what it is to exist is called Ontology. The basic idea can be summarized by thinking about our own physical existence. Intuitively we believe that before we are born we (our physical bodies) do not exist, then we exist, then after our physical death we do not exist. Life may be that simple, but there are many objections to the *not exist -> exist -> not exist* chronology.[143]

If consciousness is a physical phenomenon linked to the brain then a physical host must exist for consciousness to exist. If

---

[139] Lawrence Krauss, *A Universe from Nothing* (New York: Simon and Schuster, 2012).

[140] Thomas Sattig, *The Double Lives of Objects: An Essay in the Metaphysics of the Ordinary World* (Oxford: Oxford University Press, 2015).

[141] Willard Van Orman Quine, *Word and Object* (Cambridge: MIT Press, 2013).

[142] Eric Yang, "The Compatibility of Property Dualism and Substance Materialism," *Philosophical Studies* (2015): 1-9. doi:10.1007/s11098-015-0465-6

[143] Paul M. Churchland, *Matter and Consciousness,* (Cambridge: MIT press, 2013); Peter Van Inwagen, and Dean Zimmerman (Eds.), *Persons, Human and Divine* (Oxford: Oxford University Press, 2007).

consciousness is a physical and/or natural phenomenon linked to the mind then perhaps consciousness may exist in some permanent existential form, possibly remaining meaningful by merging into a universal panpsychic consciousness. We noted that existential consciousness is difficult to have any confidence in if for no other reason than the inevitability of conditions that will not support sentient life. Panpsychism seems almost impossible because of the diffuse nature of the proposed sentience and intuitive lack of individual self-aware consciousness.[144] However if consciousness is a non-physical phenomena, found in souls, then individual consciousness may have a unique, permanent, existence.

Ontology is the philosophic, as opposed to scientific, study of existence, of being.[145] Ontologists are deeply interested in the relationship between existence and non-existence, between something and *nothing*. The complexity of understanding the opposite natures of something and of *nothing* continues to offer support for wildly differing theories.

Since ancient times there has been a debate between *being* (οὐσία) and *becoming* (γένεσις). Plato addressed the issue by suggesting that the realm of *being* consists of things that never change, while all other things belong to becoming, things that are always changing.[146] The Greek philosopher Heraclitus thought everything is becoming, he wrote "Everything flows and nothing abides; everything gives way and nothing stays fixed. You cannot

---

144 Searle, *The Mystery of Consciousness.*
145 Ian Hacking, *Historical Ontology* (Houten: Springer Netherlands, 2002); Trenton Merricks, *Truth and Ontology* (Oxford: Clarendon Press, 2007).
146 Robert Bolton, "Plato's Distinction Between Being and Becoming," *The Review of Metaphysics* (1975): 66-95. http://www.jstor.org/stable/20126737; An excellent overview is found in Steven Savitt, "Being and Becoming in Modern Physics," *The Stanford Encyclopedia of Philosophy,* Edward N. Zalta, ed. (Summer 2014 Edition), http://plato.stanford.edu/archives/sum2014/entries/spacetime-bebecome/

step twice into the same river, for other waters are continually flowing on."[147]

The philosopher Parmenides thought otherwise: "'Is it or is it not?' Surely it is adjudged, as it needs must be, that we are to set aside the one way as unthinkable and nameless (for it is no true way), and that the other path is real and true. How, then, can what is be going to be in the future? Or how could it come into being? If it came into being, it is not; nor is it if it is going to be in the future. Thus is becoming extinguished and passing away not to be heard of. Nor is it divisible, since it is all alike, and there is no more of it in one place than in another, to hinder it from holding together, nor less of it, but everything is full of what is."[148]

The two most popular interpretations are that objects have no beginning or end, they simply exist (eternalism), and the opposite, objects come into being, exist for a finite time, and then are no more (presentism). There are many variations, including the idea that objects come into being but have no end (possibilism). We will discuss these in a later chapter. An underlying question is whether we and the objects that exist around us are permanent or temporary.[149]

You might think science favors an evolving universe where existence comes into being, but at the beginning of the 21st century most physicists think we live in a block universe[150] where there is space but nothing moves and there is time but nothing

---

[147] Philip Ellis Wheelwright, *Heraclitus* (Princeton: Princeton University Press, 1959).

[148] John Burnet, *Early Greek Philosophy* (Whitefish, MT: Kessinger Publishing, 2003).

[149] Michael Chase, "Time and Eternity from Plotinus and Boethius to Einstein." *ΣΧΟΛΗ. Философское антиковедение и классическая традиция* 1 (2014): 67-110. Available on http://www.ceeol.com

[150] Daniel Peterson and Michael Silberstein, *Relativity of Simultaneity and Eternalism: In Defense of the Block Universe* (Heidelberg: Springer Berlin, 2010). And see Christian Wuthrich, "The Fate of Presentism in Modern Physics," *arXiv preprint* (2012). http://arxiv.org/pdf/1207.1490v1.pdf Later in the book we will discuss why we favor existence presentism.

changes.[151] To illustrate some of the difficulties we will look briefly at mereology, the idea that all objects have parts, and mereological nihilism, the idea that objects with parts do not exist.

Mereology

Mereology is the common sense realization that every whole object is composed of parts which are composed of parts which are composed of parts until we reach irreducible parts called *atoms* (or simples).[152] An atom is an object (whether temporal, spatial, or point-like) that has no proper parts. The term is from the Greek word ἄτομος, meaning uncuttable or indivisible. The term was unfortunately adopted by nuclear scientists before sub-atomic particles were discovered, but for philosophers atom still means indivisible.[153]

The mereologist follows intricate rules of reflexivity, transitivity, antisymmetry, etc., to determine what a whole is and what a part is.[154] The herculean nature of this task is easily illustrated by a box of candy, which among other wholes is composed of the whole container, whole candies, whole nuts, and whole sugar molecules, all of which become different wholes as we munch. There are many different wholes to which a part may belong, the only solid rule is that a part is always less than the whole it belongs to.[155]

An example, our senses may tell us that a cat is standing in front of us. In most cases we do not think about the cat being a composite object made out of sub-atomic particles. So when is a

---

[151] Dennis Dieks, *The Ontology of Spacetime.* vol. 1. (London: Elsevier, 2006).

[152] Achille Varzi, "Mereology," *The Stanford Encyclopedia of Philosophy* (2003 Edition). http://plato.stanford.edu/entries/mereology/

[153] Alan Chalmers, *The Scientist's Atom and the Philosopher's Stone: How Science Succeeded and Philosophy Failed to Gain Knowledge of Atoms* (New York: Springer, 2009).

[154] Paul Hovda, "What is Classical Mereology?" *Journal of Philosophical Logic* 38 no. 1 (2009): 55-82. doi:10.1007/s10992-008-9092-4

[155] Jeroen Smid, "The Ontological Parsimony of Mereology," *Philosophical Studies* (2015): 1-19. doi:10.1007/s11098-015-0468-3

cat a cat? This may seem to be a trivial question, but it really is not. Is a cat a cat only if it is alive? Is it a cat at the point the first living cells divide? Is a cat a cat if it barks and chases other cats?

We might agree on an answer for the cat, but consensus quickly breaks down when we ask the question - when is a human being a human being?[156] At conception, or after three or six months of fetal development, or sometime after birth? Common sense tells us a cat is a cat even in a hat, and at some point a person is a person, but we have great difficulty explaining why we are right.[157]

Logic tells us that a composite object is "created", perhaps by observation, at a given time in a given space. But even this definition is fraught with peril, is a cat named Whiskers the same cat today as it was yesterday and as it will be tomorrow? Common sense says yes, but in fact the biologic component cells are constantly replaced and the composite is continually changing from kittenhood to old age. Should we declare a cat to be the identical same cat we saw last year, even though almost 100% of the physical parts have changed over time?[158]

This type of philosophical puzzle has existed since well before the first century. The Greek philosopher Plutarch asked if a ship belonging to Theseus was restored by replacing each and every one of its wooden parts, would it still be the same ship? Other similar puzzles include the heap, suppose that we have a heap of sand, agreeing that each grain is a part of the heap, and then we remove a grain at a time. When only one grain is left is it not true that we do not have a heap of sand? If we still have a part

---

[156] Jane English, "Abortion and the Concept of a Person," *Canadian Journal of Philosophy* 5 no. 2 (1975): 233-243. A general discussion of being written before the dialog about abortion and personhood became as morally charged.

[157] Peter Van Inwagen, *Existence: Essays in Ontology* (Cambridge: Cambridge University Press, 2014).

[158] Theodore Sider, "All the World's a Stage," *Australasian Journal of Philosophy* 74 (1996): 433-453; Megan Wallace, "Counterparts and Compositional Nihilism: A Reply to AJ Cotnoir," *Thought: A Journal of Philosophy* 2 no. 3 (2013): 242-247. doi: 10.1002/tht3.92

of what was a heap yet we do not now have a heap, how can it be true that we had a heap in the first place?

Another famous puzzle is known as the statue and the clay. Suppose on Wednesday we pass Auguste Rodin's workshop and see a pot of molten bronze on a stand. When we pass the same window on Thursday we see a statute of a man he calls the thinker. On Friday Rodin changes his mind and melts the statute turning it back to a pot of molten bronze.

The thinker was made from the bronze, so the statute is the bronze. But the thinker bears no resemblance to the molten bronze we see on Friday, so the statute is clearly not the bronze. How can the object that was on the stand be both bronze and a statute and not be a statute and bronze, how many objects existed on the stand from Wednesday to Friday if *nothing* was added or removed from the stand (if you are troubled by the pot not being present on Thursday assume the pot was bronze, was melted, poured into the statute, and then remolded on Friday)?

One solution is offered by mereological nihilism. A mereological nihilist looks at a composite whole, admits that it is made of parts, and then rejects the ontologic existence of the whole based on the fact that there are only simples in the world. This worldview solves most of the puzzles. If he or she would look at Rodin's the thinker or his pot of molten bronze, they would say that neither the statute nor the pot of bronze ever existed because only simples exist.[159]

Mereological nihilism solves all the philosophical puzzles by denying that the ship, heap, and statute ever exist. However the idea that only simples exist seems intuitively wrong. While the logic seems difficult, there are precise ways to have a cat that is not a single composite object, by saying that a cat is simples arranged cat-wise.[160] This is a good place to note that our rock is

---

[159] Theodore Sider, "Ontological Realism," *Metametaphysics* (2009): 384-423. http://tedsider.org/papers/ontological_realism.pdf
[160] Gabriele Contessa, "One's a Crowd: Mereological Nihilism Without Ordinary-Object Eliminativism," *Analytic Philosophy* (2014). http://philpapers.org/rec/CONOAC

a real object whether it is our pet rock, or an assembly of simples arranged pet rock-wise.

More recently philosophers have been considering linguistics, semantics, and cognitive science in an attempt to understand objects.[161] The interest comes from the argument that our pet rock does not know it is a rock, only a conscious being can have that knowledge. Like the dedicated scrabble player, we have used our alphabet to construct a lot of words which in turn build a maze of both related and unrelated semantic concepts. The philosopher Friederike Moltmann explains the relationship between linguistic semantics and descriptive metaphysics.[162] He provides an excellent summary of the many dark alleys that linguistics can lead us into when we seek to define existence and its opposites.

One of the dead-end alleys is solipsism, the extreme metaphysical position that the world and other minds do not exist.[163] The epistemological version is the less dramatic perspectivism, we cannot directly know the reality of anything because everything we know is passed through the mind, linguistics, etc. In other words every sensory input is uniquely interpreted by our consciousness. It is the dilemma of two people eating a piece of chocolate, one says to the other this is the best chocolate in the world. The other person, a philosopher, sadly realizes that he or she can never know exactly how the chocolate tastes to his or her friend. This is the essence of perspectivism.

It seems that even the extreme view of solipsism will remain a possibility because if all that we experience is an illusion, we will be unable to prove, or for that matter disprove, that fact from outside the illusion.[164] Indeed quantum theory

---

[161] Roderick Chisholm, *Person and Object: A Metaphysical Study*. (London: Routledge, 2014).

[162] Friederike Moltmann, "The Semantics of Existence." *Linguistics and Philosophy* 36 no. 1 (2013): 31-63. doi: 10.1007/s10988-013-9127-3

[163] Richard A. Watson, *Solipsism: The Ultimate Empirical Theory of Human Existence* (South Bend, IN: St Augustine Press, 2015).

[164] Proponents of idealism and similar philosophies believe that consciousness is all there is and that the material world is an illusion.

lends support to the extreme solipsist[165] and perhaps to the futility of philosophy. We can find comfort in John Searle's comment "It is a use-mention fallacy to suppose that the linguistic and conceptual nature of the identification of a fact requires that the fact identified be itself linguistic in nature. Facts are conditions that make statements true, but they are not identical with their linguistic descriptions. We invent words to state facts and to name things, but it does not follow that we invent the facts or the things."[166]

Why should all of this be of interest to us? One of the methods by which philosophers seek to understand *nothing* is by the subtraction principal. Basically if there are n number of objects in the world then *nothing* is when $n = 0$. Therefore what an object and what a simple is becomes of significance.

We do not need to engage in the ongoing lively debates about mereology, but we will look at the final step, when we have $n = 1$. What does it mean to say *nothing* $= n - 1$? In other words, if there is only one simple left in the world, can we subtract that simple from the world?[167] Philosophers do not agree on an

---

We consider idealism to be a highly unlikely possibility. Terry Pinkard, *German Philosophy 1760-1860: the Legacy of Idealism.* (Cambridge: Cambridge University Press, 2002); Immanuel Kant, *Critique of Pure Reason,* eds. Paul Guyer and Allen W. Wood (Cambridge: Cambridge University Press, 1999); Henry E. Allison, *Kant's Transcendental Idealism* (New Haven: Yale University Press, 2004).

[165] Amanda Gefter, *Trespassing on Einstein's Lawn: A Father, a Daughter, the Meaning of Nothing, and the Beginning of Everything* (New York: Random House, 2014). An easy to read description of what one might call quantum solipsism. See also - Max Tegmark, *Our Mathematical Universe: My Quest for the Ultimate Nature of Reality* (New York: Random House, 2014).

[166] John R. Searle, *Mind, Language and Society: Philosophy in the Real World* (New York: Basic Books, 1998): 22.

[167] D. Efird, and T. Stoneham, "Justifying Metaphysical Nihilism: a response to Cameron," *The Philosophical Quarterly* 59 (2009): 132–37, but see A. Paseau, "Why the Subtraction Argument Does Not Add Up," *Analysis* 62 (2002): 73–75.
http://www.jstor.org/discover/10.2307/3329071

answer, we will reserve judgment until we look more closely at the concept of *nothing*.

Physicalism

Having looked at mereology, we are going to jump to questions about the existence of objects that are composed of many parts. We need to understand two concepts, property dualism and substance dualism. But first we need a short definition of physicalism,[168] which is similar to materialism[169] and is a companion of the naturalist approach.[170]

Physicalism argues that it is true that everything is physical, that there is nothing which is non-physical.[171] Physicalism is divided into *a priori* and *a posteriori* physicalism. Basically if the truth of physicalism is deduced from the nature of the physical world, if the inference is independent of experience, it is *a priori*. If the inference of physicalism is determined by or dependent on experience it is *a posteriori*. The view of

---

[168] David Papineau, "The Rise of Physicalism." In Carl Gillett & Barry M. Loewer, eds., *Physicalism and its Discontents* (Cambridge: Cambridge University Press, 2001); Derk Pereboom, *Consciousness and the Prospects of Physicalism* (Oxford: Oxford University Press, 2011).
[169] Philosophical monism states that matter is fundamental, and that all phenomena are the result of interactions involving matter. Joseph Levine, "Materialism and Qualia: The Explanatory Gap," *Pacific Philosophical Quarterly* 64, no. 4 (1983): 354-361.
[170] Roy Bhaskar, *A Possibility of Naturalism: A Philosophical Critique of the Contemporary Human Sciences.* (London: Routledge, 2014); Ted Benton, "Some Comments on Roy Bhaskar's 'The Possibility of Naturalism'," In *Critical Realism: Essential Readings* 27 (2013), 297; Alvin Plantinga, *Where the Conflict Really Lies: Science, Religion, and Naturalism* (Oxford: Oxford University Press, 2011); Jack Ritchie, *Understanding Naturalism* (London: Routledge, 2014).
[171] Physicalism, Property Dualism, and Substance Dualism are philosophic companions of Stuart Hameroff's scientific classifications.

physicalism as *a priori*[172] or *a posteriori*[173] affects how logical challenges to it are presented.

The underlying question is whether there can be experience in a totally physical world. Physicalism is a metaphysical framework on which mind / brain / body problems are considered, it denies the existence of a metaphysical mind. There are strong supporters of physicalism,[174] but the alternatives to physicalism have an equal or greater number of followers.[175] The usual argument against physicalism / materialism is based on some form of dualism.[176]

Property Dualism

Property dualism accepts that our mind has immaterial, non-physical, properties, but does not accept that human beings have immaterial souls separate from our bodies.[177] It recognizes

---

[172] Philip Goff, "A Priori Physicalism, Lonely Ghosts and Cartesian Doubt." *Consciousness and Cognition* 21 no. 2 (2012): 742-746. doi:10.1016/j.concog.2011.02.007

[173] Philip Goff, "A Posteriori Physicalists Get Our Phenomenal Concepts Wrong," *Australasian Journal of Philosophy* 89 no. 2 (2011): 191-209. doi:10.1080/00048401003649617; E. Diaz-Leon, "Do a Posteriori Physicalists Get Our Phenomenal Concepts Wrong?" *Ratio* 27 no. 1 (2014): 1-16. doi:10.1111/rati.12018

[174] David Papineau, "What Exactly is the Explanatory Gap?" *Philosophia* 39 no. 1 (2011): 5-19. doi:10.1007/s11406-010-9273-6

[175] Joseph A. Baltimore, "Careful, Physicalists: Mind–Body Supervenience Can Be Too Superduper." *Theoria* 79 no. 1 (2013): 8-21. doi:10.1111/j.1755-2567.2012.01140.x; Benedikt Paul Gocke, *After Physicalism* (Notre Dame: Univ. of Notre Dame Press, 2012).

[176] Van Inwagen, and Zimmerman (Eds.), *Persons, Human and Divine*. As of 2015 this excellent book was available from http://michaelsudduth.com/wp-content/uploads/2013/04/vanInwagen-Persons-Human-and-Divine.pdf, it is recommended, especially the introduction, as a clear summary of the philosophy of mind / brain / body.

[177] John Foster, *The Immaterial Self: A Defence of the Cartesian Dualist Conception of the Mind.* (London: Routledge, 2002); Max Velmans, *Understanding Consciousness.*

physicalism[178]/ materialism as the proper way of understanding the source of non-physical consciousness. You may ask how can any philosophy that incorporates non-physical properties coexist with physicalism?

The answer is that something called token physicalism[179] is called upon to avoid contradicting the principal that causation consistent with science requires physical mechanisms. "Token" does not mean a less than real physicalism, it implies that every particular thing is in fact a physical particular. In other words it allows for non-physical mental properties contingently related to the physical brain / body. A property dualist asserts that when matter is organized in the way that human bodies are organized (a mereologist might say simples arranged human-wise), the non-physical mental properties emerge from, and are contingent on, the physical.[180]

Substance Dualism

Substance dualism says that the mind and the body are different substances, and that the mind has immaterial, non-physical, properties, including the property of not being constrained to follow the laws of physics.[181] Even though the mind is independent of the brain and is said to be able to exist even if the brain does not, it does not necessarily follow that human beings are immaterial souls[182] that exist apart from our

---

[178] Jaegwon Kim, *Physicalism, or Something Near Enough* (Princeton: Princeton University Press, 2007); Daniel Stoljar, *Physicalism* (London: Routledge, 2010).
[179] Jerry A. Fodor, " Special Sciences or: The Disunity of Science as a Working Hypothesis." *Synthese* 28, no. 2 (1974): 97-115; Noa Latham, "What is Token Physicalism?" *Pacific Philosophical Quarterly* 84, no. 3 (2003): 270-290. doi:10.1111/1468-0114.00173
[180] Jennifer Hornsby, "Which physical events are mental events?" In *Proceedings of the Aristotelian Society* (1980): 73-92. http://www.jstor.org/stable/4544966
[181] Van Inwagen and Zimmerman (Eds.), *Persons, Human and Divine.*
[182] Stewart Goetz and Charles Taliaferro. *A Brief History of the Soul* (Hoboken: John Wiley and Sons, 2011).

physical bodies.[183] Dualists agree that human beings are both material and immaterial beings, but they are divided as to whether a "person" is an entirely immaterial occupant of a physical body, or is both a material and an immaterial being.

The dualism of mind and brain creates an immediate problem, how can the non-physical mind violate physical laws and *cause* physical events, and still be consistent with science? There are several schools of substance dualist thought based on the causal sequence of events that try to answer the question by explaining how the mind and the brain do or do not interact. Interactionists simply accept that the mind and brain interact with each other, but this begs the question how can we reconcile causation between the subjective non-physical and the objective (scientific) physical? Occasionalists try to coexist with physical science by attributing interactions between mind / brain / body to God as the ultimate cause of all events (whether directly or through laws of nature), in other words God is the cause of all changes in the world so there are no conflicting causes.

Epiphenomenalists fall somewhere in-between, asserting that the brain / body can affect the mind but that the non-physical mind cannot affect the brain / body, thus isolating the non-physical from violating physical laws. Yet our intuition tells us that physical events like seeing a beautiful sunset cause a pleasant non-physical mental experience which in turn causes a physical smile. Peter Unger is a strong supporter of substance dualism,[184] however many objections remain.[185] It is fair to say that none of the dualist, or for that matter monist, approaches have solved the philosophical problems associated with the non-physical.

While most substance dualists accept that the mind / soul outlives the body, substance dualism does not require that

---

183 Foster, *The Immaterial Self: A Defence of the Cartesian Dualist Conception of the Mind*; Max Velmans, *Understanding Consciousness*.
184 Peter Unger, "The Survival of the Sentient," *Noûs* 34 no. s14 (2000): 325-348. DOI: 10.1111/0029-4624.34.s14.17; Peter K. Unger, *All the Power in the World* (Oxford: Oxford University Press, 2006).
185 Will Bynoe and Nicholas K. Jones, "Solitude Without Souls: Why Peter Unger Hasn't Established Substance Dualism," *Philosophia* 41 (2013): 109-125. doi:10.1007/s11406-012-9384-3

conclusion. Arguably those who believe in existence of consciousness after physical death are necessarily substance dualists, but not all substance dualists must believe in life after physical death. For our purposes we place substance dualists who believe in natural laws that are a fundamental part of the universe and which govern the immaterial mind in our physical / natural consciousness – independent classification. Those who call themselves substance dualists, and who believe in some form of permanent immaterial consciousness not constrained by physical and natural laws are assigned to our classification non-physical consciousness - independent. Our main concern is not whether we have a material brain and an immaterial mind, we are primarily interested in whether human consciousness has a finite existence or not.

Revisiting Mereology

We briefly return to mereology and see how well it fits with dualism. The argument of mereology says that if there is a cloud with a water drop on the right side and a water drop on the left side, we must be able to say that there exists a cloud that contains the left water drop but not the right and there exists a cloud that contains the right water drop but not the left, and that both are an object that is a cloud. We can divide the parts of a single cloud into many configurations, and we can have many clouds, yet taken all together there is still a unitary cloud.

A car is a car so long as it has car like parts, a human being is a human being because he or she exhibits a set of human like parts called cells arranged human-wise. It would be comforting to be able to cite articles that define human existence, but we are in an area of discomfort even for philosophers. Most philosophers accept mereology and agree that which is a human being is distinct from that which is a human being plus an additional atom, cell, etc. This results in an enormous number of physical, material, objects that are unique human beings, being located in roughly the same space, each having only a tiny bit different components from the others.

A primary argument for an independent soul hinges on the fact that mereology tells us that if you sit down in a chair there is not one, but many, physical human beings sitting in the chair. Yet there is only one event that all the human beings in the chair experience. So mereologists and dualists might say that there are also many *experiencers*, one for each human being.

But we intuitively know that there is only one subject (thing with a conscious mental life) that experiences pain and joy for all of the overlapping physical human beings. So a group of experiencers won't work, because there is only one subject that experiences the event. The answer substance dualists give is that the human beings are not unique but that they embody souls which are unique.

The arguments go like this:

(1) If Materialism (Physicalism) is true, then many subjects are in your chair.

(2) Uniqueness is true.

(3) So Materialism is false (there is no single subject who experiences events).

"Everyone should agree that (at least usually) a subject has a special relationship with a particular material object, presumably a human: the properties of the subject and material object [human body] systematically co-vary such that it's appropriate to say that the latter 'is the body of' the former. For example, dropping a book on your toe results in your feeling pain, and deciding to make a cup of tea results in your body rising from its seat."[186] Bynoe and Jones call this *embodiment*, so we need to talk about properties that material objects [human bodies] embody subjects with and properties that subjects impart upon the material objects.

Unger's argument[187] for a dualist soul is simplified in this manner:

If Subjects satisfy Embodiment and almost materially coincide then -
for Uniqueness to be satisfied:

---

[186] Bynoe and Jones, "Solitude Without Souls," 6.
[187] Unger, "The Survival of the Sentient,"; Unger, *All the Power in the World*.

No human in your chair embodies more than one Subject, and no two of them embody distinct Subjects.[188]

Unger argues that if materialism is true then for Uniqueness to be satisfied each human in the chair must causally interact with a soul that embodies the Subject. For Uniqueness to be satisfied:

No Subject causally promotes more than one soul, and no two of them causally promote distinct souls.[189]

This allows human beings who are made up of multiple parts to have one mind / soul. From this logic Unger builds a case that the experiencer must be an independent soul and that the problem of the many dictates that substance dualism must be true, therefore we have a non-physical soul.

Bynoe and Jones take the same approach as Unger and agree that in any chair in which you sit there are many human beings. They then associate a material Experiencer / Subject with each human being, and state –

No human in your chair is amongst more than one plurality of collective subjects, and no two of those humans are amongst distinct pluralities of collective subjects.[190]

If you want to consider some of the difficulties that philosophers have in understanding mind and brain / body consciousness and existence, you may want to read Will Bynoe and Nicholas Jones (2013) "Solitude Without Souls: Why Peter Unger Hasn't Established Substance Dualism". Their response to Unger's philosophical argument for substance dualism, for existence of a soul, shows both how difficult the topic is and perhaps how unsatisfactory semantics can be. The basic point is that for Bynoe and Jones the *experiencer* is a material plural, a collection of physical parts that act together as a single mind. Bynoe and Jones admit that neither their physicalist / materialist approach nor the dualist's arguments solve the hard problems of mind, brain, and

---

[188] Ibid.
[189] Bynoe and Jones, "Solitude Without Souls," 8.
[190] Ibid.

body.[191] Both philosophers and scientists continue to search for answers.[192]

There are many controversial variations on dualism and similar ideas, including ontological emergence [the whole is more than the sum of its parts, it has emergent properties].[193] Where physicalists think that all properties supervene with metaphysical necessity on physical properties and laws, emergentists hold that there are emergent properties that supervene only with nomological (not theoretically explicable) necessity on physical properties and laws. They argue that this is true because emergent laws like physical laws need to be fixed in order to produce emergent properties.

Mereological nihilism does not help us much with our quest,[194] are there other more fundamental onotologic theories that might be of assistance, such as Metaontology?[195] Metaontology is the study of what ontology is, what is the question ontology is trying to answer. It may lead to an understanding of the metaphysical difficulties that keep popping up. If you have the interest needed to delve deeply into

---

[191] John Horgan, "David Chalmers Thinks the Hard Problem Is Really Hard," *Scientific American*, April 2017; Michael Graziano, *Rethinking Consciousness* (W. W. Norton & Company, 2019).

[192] John Horgan, "David Chalmers Thinks the Hard Problem Is Really Hard," *Scientific American*, April 2017; Michael Graziano, *Rethinking Consciousness* (W. W. Norton & Company, 2019).

[193] Peter Fazekas, "Pursuing Natural Piety: Understanding Ontological Emergence and Distinguishing it from Physicalism," *Dialectica* 68 (2014): 97-119. doi:10.1111/1746-8361.12056

[194] Jonah Goldwater, "No Composition, No Problem: Ordinary Objects as Arrangements," *Philosophia* (2015): 1-13. doi:10.1007/s11406-015-9593-7

[195] Peter Van Inwagen, "Meta-ontology," *Erkenntnis* 48 (1998): 233-250. Retrieved May 5, 2015 from http://www.andrewmbailey.com/pvi/Meta-ontology.pdf; Matti Eklund, "Metaontology," *Philosophy Compass* 1 no. 3 (2006): 317-334. doi:10.1111/j.1747-9991.2006.00026.x

epistemology and ontology, Jason Turner carefully reviews the landscape.[196]

The End of Philosophy?

The current state of knowledge perhaps suggests that there is more than the physical / material in the universe, and that both science and philosophy are recognizing the shadows of a non-physical realm. The non-physical may or may not be related to dark energy, quantum gravity, non-locality, vacuum ether, souls, after-life, etc. Why did we go to so much effort to present the debate between mind and brain, property dualists and substance dualists? The reason we must admit was less to illuminate the discussion than to point out the state of turmoil that both philosophy and science are in when it comes to consciousness and existence.

Mathematics is the language of science, semantics is the language of philosophy. Most physicists believe that the current understanding of mathematics is inadequate to answer questions about reality. It is assumed that the temporal framework of quantum theory is incompatible with relativity, and that if quantum gravity is ever understood it will introduce us to new physics and math.

Like the physicists, some philosophers have recognized that language and semantics may not be sufficient to logically solve their problems. They have found that necessary semantic tools are missing. We may be wrong, but the logical arguments that philosophers are offering seem less than helpful toward understanding mind / brain / body realities.

From the perspective of philosophers there have been politically incorrect, but objectively interesting, declarations by

---

[196] Jason Turner, "Are Ontological Debates Defective." Online article. (2011). http://www.slu.edu/~turnerjt/papers/Defective-web.pdf

scientists, including Neil deGrasse Tyson,[197] Michio Kaku,[198] and Stephen Hawking, that philosophy has no place in the modern world.[199] Yet our favorite physicist, Carlo Rovelli, is a strong supporter of philosophical inquiry.[200] Similarly there have been numerous protestations by philosophers against scientists who proclaim the truth of theories that have not been, or cannot be, verified by experiment.[201]

Our position is not to be too critical of science or philosophy. We simply recognize that at the start of the third millennium that philosophy has not been able to answer fundamental metaphysical questions and science has not been able to answer fundamental physical questions about human consciousness and existence. We would argue that unless and

---

[197] "No, I'm so disappointed with philosophy. Philosophy in the twenty first century, philosophy conducted by philosophers who were trained in the twentieth century have made, as far as I've been able to judge have made no contributions to the advance of our understanding of our physical universe." N. D. Tyson, (2009).
http://www.haydenplanetarium.org/tyson/read/2009/07/23/called -by-the-universe

[198] Michio Kaku, *The Future of the Mind: The Scientific Quest to Understand, Enhance, and Empower the Mind* (New York: Doubleday, 2014). See also Tim Dean, "The Mind of Michio Kaku," *Cosmos* (July 21, 2014). https://cosmosmagazine.com/life-sciences/mind-michio-kaku

[199] Stephen Hawking with Leonard Mlodinow, *The Grand Design: New Answers to the Ultimate Questions of Life* (New York: Bantam Press, 2010); C. Norris, "Hawking Contra Philosophy," *Philosophy Now* 82 (2011): 21-24.
https://philosophynow.org/issues/82/Hawking_contra_Philosophy.

[200] Carlo Rovelli, "Aristotle's Physics: A Physicist's Look," *Journal of the American Philosophical Association* 1 (2015):23-40.
doi:10.1017/apa.2014.11

[140] George Ellis and Joe Silk, "Scientific Method: Defend the Integrity of Physics," *Nature* 516 no. 7531 (2014): 321-323.
doi:10.1038/516321a; Melanie Frappier, Letitia Meynell, and James Robert Brown, eds. *Thought Experiments in Science, Philosophy, and the Arts* (London: Routledge, 2012); Clark Glymour, Richard Scheines and Peter Spirtes, *Discovering Causal Structure: Artificial Intelligence, Philosophy of Science, and Statistical Modeling*, Originally published 1987. (Waltham: Academic Press, 2014).

until there are breakthroughs in science and philosophy, it is rational and logical to give weight to intuitive beliefs about consciousness and existence.

Back to our cat (from the Philosophy chapters), common sense tells us that from some point after conception to some point before death we can say with reasonable confidence that Whiskers is a single living cat. Now our intuition tells us it is true that at some time before the event of being born Whiskers was not a cat, and that at some time after he dies Whiskers will not be a cat. Parmenides recognized the difficulty with using tensed language, such as *before* and *after*, to describe physical states that are not part of our only intuitive reality, the present.[202]

While we might open the ontological existential can of worms as to what it means to exist, at least for the moment we will accept that while alive Whiskers the cat exists, and that before birth and after death he does not exist. We will return to questions about the block universe and non-physical consciousness later in the book. We assume that whether or not we conjugate our verbs, when asked does Whiskers exist, an objective observer will intuitively say that he does not exist, does exist, does not exist in that sequential order.

Whether or not our intuition matches reality is not known. We are not trying to definitively answer the question does anything exist, or the question is it possible for *nothing* to exist, we are simply suggesting that for object X, in our case a cat, X does not exist, X does exist, X does not exist. To make our examples more personal let's look at human beings instead of a cat.[203]

---

[202] Burnet, 126.

[203] Saul A. Kripke, *Reference and Existence: The John Locke Lectures* (Oxford: Oxford University Press, 2013); Stephen Mulhall, *On Being in the World: Wittgenstein and Heidegger on Seeing Aspects* (London: Routledge, 2014); Richard Polt, "Being and Time," In *Martin Heidegger: Key Concepts* (London: Routledge, 2014): 69-81.

Physical Death

What if materialists, rationalists, naturalists, physicalists, property dualists, and everyone else who believes that consciousness is dependent on our physical bodies, that the mind is a product of our biologic brain, are right? What if when the brain ceases to function the mind disappears? There certainly is a common sense intuitive feeling that the human skeleton in the museum does not think about the people who come to visit. Our pet rock feels no pain.

Philosophers often speak of the void that would follow physical death without life after death as the abyss, the unknown, the approaching void, etc. All of these suggest that we are on a journey to a place which lies at the end of our physical lifetimes. If on our death we cease to exist, this idea that we are traveling to our ultimate destiny is false. We are not traveling to an abyss, the void, or the unknown, for these words suggest that we are moving toward something. If there is no non-physical existence then on the death of each of us, *nothing*.

As we said earlier, the fact that you are moving steadily toward your death is most likely, and literally, to be the last thing on your mind.[204] Observing the inevitable death of every creature that inhabits the earth, we may have a recurrent feeling that death is the end.[205] On the other hand, it is virtually inconceivable to us that all we are, all we have been, all we will be, may be rendered void in that moment of death.[206]

It goes against human nature to visualize the effective destruction of our past, present, and future, which may accompany death without existence beyond death. Yet if each human being does cease to exist, then all human beings are, or in the case of generations yet unborn will be, waiting their turn to

---

[204] Robert Kastenbaum, *The Psychology of Death* (New York: Springer Publishing Company, 2000); Steven Luper, *The Philosophy of Death* (Cambridge: Cambridge University Press, 2009). Both of these books fail to address *nothing*, which we will attempt to do.
[205] Jonathon Brown, *The Self* (New York: Psychology Press, 2014).
[206] Ernest Becker, *The Denial of Death* (New York: Simon and Schuster, 2007).

cease existing. If each and every human being ceases to be, then the feeling of continuity that pervades the human race may be false. Please note, as we discuss later and in our book LifeNotes (http://www.LifeNotes.org), we do not believe that life is in fact destroyed by physical death.

If in fact you are conscious and you do exercise meaningful freedom of choice, what good is it to be a unique human being if at your death you cease to exist? If you do not continue to exist in some form after death, what good are all the experiences, decisions, triumphs, defeats, all the moments of your life? If you do not survive the grave, if you return to the state of being that preceded your birth, then perhaps nothing in fact does matter.

While over the ages men and women have sought to perpetuate themselves through their children, their place in history, their role in society, and through intricate philosophical webs of existentialism[207] and other essays on physical man's importance, the fact of physical death remains. If each generation's death means the end of those individuals, then we are all faced with an endless cycle of creation and destruction, the meaning of which, if any, is beyond comprehension.

In their arguments for humanism, existentialism, etc., philosophers have spent lifetimes trying to construct a difference between the apparent continuity of humankind,[208] and the periodic death of individual humans.[209] Most of us think of our ancestors as a link to the past, and our children as a link to the

---

[207] William Barrett, *Irrational Man: A Study in Existential Philosophy* (Hamburg: Anchor, 2011); Robert G. Olson, *An Introduction to Existentialism* (N. Chelmsford: Courier Corporation, 2012).
[208] Peter L Berger, *The Sacred Canopy: Elements of a Sociological Theory of Religion* (New York: Open Road Media, 2011).
[209] Martin Heidegger, *Being and Time: A Translation of Sein und Zeit* (Albany: SUNY Press, 1996); Karl Jaspers, *Way to Wisdom: An Introduction to Philosophy* (Princeton: Yale University Press, 1971); Robert Jay Lifton, *The Broken Connection: on Death And the Continuity of Life* (Arlington: American Psychiatric Publishers, 1996); Filiz Peach, "Death, Faith and Existentialism," *Philosophy Now* 27 (2000): 12-14. https://philosophynow.org/issues/27/Death_Faith_and_Existentialism

future, yet if we do not survive the grave each generation may die an isolated death that mocks any assertion that humankind has a continuing existence apart from its individual members. If each person's death results in their no longer existing, then no manner of historical recording, social progression, or other remembrance in the minds of those whose time to die is yet to come, can in any way affect, preserve, or make any difference whatsoever to those who no longer are. No one will survive to remember. If each of us ceases to be, then your life may have no meaning and your choices may make no difference.

We admit that this logic seems counter intuitive, and even wrong, but if we are willing to dissociate ourselves from the incredible biologic urge for self-preservation, both of the individual and the species, and are willing to apply purely objective reasoning, the logical conclusions, while discomforting, are perhaps inevitable (we will discuss several possible logical loopholes like the block universe, interpretations of existentialism, etc., that might give permanent meaning and value to a finite physical life). This is a very difficult conclusion to accept, it goes against our intuitive feelings about the continuity of human life, and against our assumptions that individual physical lives have some kind of meaning and value.

Yet if we are little more than doomed animals, our intuitive feeling of meaning and value would not be surprising. From the very beginning, to assure survival of any species, evolution would certainly have instilled in living creatures the feeling that there is a reason for them to exist, a reason for them to crawl out of the ocean and build cities. If there is no life after death, and our lives are in fact consumed by *nothing*, it is no wonder that our genetic heritage argues so strongly against that possibility.

Because it is so difficult to accept, we will consider our conclusion in more intuitive detail. To keep things simple we will discuss physical consciousness, but please realize that what we say about the material brain applies equally to any consciousness of an immaterial mind constrained by natural laws (a separate mind that is dependent on a brain for its existence). However, our discussion does not apply to non-physical consciousness that is not dependent on the existence of a brain / mind. Therefore,

75

what we say about physical death applies equally to physical / natural death, whether natural death occurs at the moment of physical death or some finite time after physical death.

It seems logical to assume that if each person's consciousness is the product of their physical bodies, then individual physical consciousness exists only during that person's physical life on earth, plus perhaps a finite period allowed by natural laws.[210] If each of our physical lives proceeds from birth to death, then the consequence of each person's death necessarily follows their death.

Who can be affected by that death? Certainly those who survive may be affected, but here is the problem, the death cannot be of any consequence to the purely physical human being who no longer exists! The moment before the death of a human being it can be said that their impending death affects them, but the very moment after the person dies, he or she is no longer around to be affected!

Most agree that cause and effect, action and consequence, occur in a fixed order, the former always preceding the latter.[211] Let us assume, for example, that a comet collides with the Earth at some time in the future before humans have colonized space.

----

[210] We are highly skeptical of the existence of natural laws that are fundamentally separate from physical laws, that are constrained as a part of the universe, and that supervene on the physical. If there are such natural laws, our material brain is constrained by physical laws and our immaterial mind is constrained by natural laws. Both physical and natural laws intuitively place an absolute limit on the continued existence of consciousness. In other words, the posited natural laws do not appear capable of providing individual human beings with a permanent consciousness.

[211] Atanu Chatterjee, "Causality: Physics and Philosophy," *European Journal of Physics Education* 4 no. 2 (2012). http://ejpe.erciyes.edu.tr/index.php/EJPE/article/view/80; Steven A. Sloman and David Lagnado. "Causality in Thought," *Annual Review of Psychology* 66 (2015): 223-247. doi:10.1146/annurev-psych-010814-015135; T. N. Palmer, "Lorenz, Gödel and Penrose: New Perspectives on Determinism and Causality in Fundamental Physics," *Contemporary Physics* 55 no. 3 (2014): 157-178. Palmer may not be right but the idea is interesting. http://arxiv.org/pdf/1309.2396v2.pdf

Assume further that all life on Earth is annihilated by the collision. It is very hard to accept, but if consciousness, our mind, is nothing more than a physical / natural phenomena, if there is no non-physical continuation of life after death, then the most logical conclusion is that the complete annihilation of humankind is of absolutely no consequence to humankind! While the words may sound bizarre and counter intuitive, in fact they may not be. The moment after the total destruction of humankind it can be said with some certainty that the destruction of humankind had no effect whatsoever on humankind, simply because humankind no longer exists to be affected.

If you accept that time has direction (we believe that even absent a fundamental time, all events follow a causal, sequential, chain), then cause and effect, action and consequence, occur in a fixed order, the former always preceding the latter.[212] Keeping that in mind, the idea that after the total destruction of humankind there would be no one left to be affected should not seem as bizarre. Assuming that one event will always precede another event in order of occurrence, if the event that is called the death of a human being is equivalent to the physical[213] annihilation of that human being, the consequence of the event necessarily follows the event. If there is a causal sequence to events, then the annihilation cannot be of any consequence to a human being who no longer exists (you should be aware that our conclusions about physical annihilation are often rejected by those who believe we live in some kind of block universe).

---

[212] Časlav Brukner, "Quantum Causality." *Nature Physics* 10 no. 4 (2014): 259-263. doi: 10.1038/NPHYS2930; Paul Davies, "That Mysterious Flow," *Scientific American* 23 (2014): 8-13. doi:10.1038/scientificamericantime1114-8

[213] The idea that the mind is a different substance to the brain raises the possibility that the immaterial "natural" should be considered as having a parallel existence to the physical. That does not change the fact that if the natural is part of the universe and subject to natural laws, it is intuitively true that it is subject to annihilation (even if not simultaneous) just as the physical is. Because we do not understand the immaterial laws of nature, we can do no more than accept this conclusion as intuitively being the most likely possibility.

Again, the moment before the destruction of humankind perhaps it could be said that the impending destruction affects humankind, but the very moment after humankind is destroyed there is absolutely no humankind left to be affected. Assume that the comet annihilates humankind at 12:00 noon, the consequence of that destruction occurs at 12:00 noon PLUS a moment in time, and at 12:00 noon plus the moment in time there is no humankind left to be affected. Indeed, there is no humankind around that is conscious of the fact that the comet struck the earth!

The same logic applies to the history of individuals not visited by a catastrophic event. If you believe that each human being is nothing more than an individual physical entity, and therefore that there is no life after death, then at the time of their death each human being experiences the identical individual annihilation that all humankind would experience together if the earth and its inhabitants were simultaneously destroyed. If a human being dies at 12:00 noon, and there is no life after death, at 12:01 they are not around to be affected by their death.

If an individual named Bill dies at 12:00 noon, at 12:01 Bill no longer exists to be affected by his death. If Bill is a purely physical entity that does not survive death, after 12:00 noon (i.e. - after completion of the sequence of causal events that precede Bill's death) you could search the entire universe for Bill and you would not find him (some readers are probably thinking that Bill continues to exist as his worldline in a block universe even after his physical death, we discuss that later). Bill's death occurs at precisely 12:00 noon. Not minutes, or even moments, later. If there is no life after death, the very moment after the event known as Bill's death, Bill no longer exists.[214] After 12:00 noon Bill cannot be affected by anything, including his death.

Past, Present, and Future

The logic goes even further. If you do not believe that human consciousness continues to exist after physical death, then death not only annihilates each individual's present and future,

---

[214] E. J. Lowe, *The Possibility of Metaphysics* (Oxford: Clarendon, 1998),137-138.

but also annihilates their past.[215] Most people would agree that for an object to have a present and a future the object must exist. Yet many would make the distinction that while an object cannot have a present and a future if it does not exist, it somehow can have a past.

It is clear that the present and future of an object are bound to the existence of the object, but so too is the object's past. Much of the problem lies in the use of the words past, present, and future both to describe that which is part of an object (a "past" that belongs to the object, like a person's memories that belong to the living individual from birth to death), and to describe the existence of the object from a third party's view (a "past" which is a chronological description of an object, like a photo album containing a lifetime collection of pictures of an individual who has died).

It is a misconception to equate the fact that there is a "history" of all beings or objects that is set in the "past", with the statement that a being or object that no longer exists has a "past". The first idea simply says that the being or object existed over a finite period that is apparent to those who currently exist. The extension of the concept of such a history to the idea that somehow the object or being that no longer exists still possesses a "past" confuses the distinction these two words can convey.

Once an object or being no longer exists it obviously has no present or future, similarly the object has no past. While it may be difficult to accept, a mountain that no longer exists has no past, present, or future for the simple reason that there is no such mountain.[216] There is a current history of a mountain that once

---

[215] Jonathan Charles Tallant, "Defining Existence Presentism," *Erkenntnis* 79 (2014): 479-501. doi:10.1007/s10670-013-9499-3 Tallant's concept of existence presentism is very close to our philosophical and scientific views.

[216] Francesco Berto, *Existence as a Real Property: The Ontology of Meinongianism* (New York: Springer Science & Business Media, 2012). Note that Meinongianism is about things that do not exist, we reference Berto's article as a good summary of the problem of non-existent things. A Meinongian might take a realist perspective toward

existed, but there is no mountain we can point to and describe the past of. This is far more than semantics. A person who lived a thousand years ago had a historic life that those who are alive can be conscious of, but the person no longer has a past that is their past, which they can be conscious of.

This logic seems wrong, in part because we celebrate the lives of famous politicians, scientists, and others who made positive contributions to society as if their deeds impart value and meaning on their lives both before and after physical death. Physicians who generations ago discovered treatments for smallpox and polio, saving millions of lives, are honored by the living as if they are still vaccinating children. We act as if our memory of a famous person is the living person.

Yet the famous people we commemorate exist only in our memory and on the pages of our history books, they do not exist as human beings. Because they do not exist, they cannot possess anything. They have no memories, no accomplishments, no rewards, they have *nothing*.

The English language lacks the words that would make it easy to convey the difference between a "history" set in the past that is the sum of all lifetimes, and a "past" that is unique to and dependent on the existence of an individual life. Perhaps humankind has avoided the initially discomforting possibility of finite pasts by not distinguishing them from the infinite. Perhaps the majority simply do not accept the possibility of the perpetual annihilation of human beings.

Admittedly, our conclusions about physical death are totally opposite to our common sense understanding of life [again, if you find yourself distressed or depressed by our conclusions please finish reading this book and read the Appendix]. Virtually everyone is certain, for example, that if they are eleven years old, and therefore have already experienced

---

the mountain that once existed or might take the constructivist view that existence of the mountain is in your mind (a technical Meinongian might say *there is* an x such that Mountain x and Existed x are true). This does not weaken our intuitive realist argument that after a mountain collapses there is no mountain that we can physically point to as an object and say that mountain had a past.

their tenth birthday, nothing can take away from them the past experience of being ten years old.

It is this assumption, that our past somehow exists forever, that is at the heart of all humanistic belief systems, including those arising out of neuro-existentialism. Indeed, belief in some kind of persistence of a human being's past is the only rational argument for the universal humanistic conclusion that even if physical death is the end, living a good life gives meaning and value to human existence. However, there is a problem with the humanist's view.

Humanist philosophers seem to accept that human consciousness is purely physical, or at least is dependent on physical / natural laws for continued existence, and acknowledge the end of consciousness at (or some finite time after) physical death. Yet almost all modern humanist philosophers tell us that a finite life can have meaning and value. The problem lies in failure to accept the rational and logical possible consequences for each human being if individual consciousness ceases to exist on the physical death of the mind and body. Humanist philosophers either ignore[217] or misunderstand what the future may hold for us after physical death if we are nothing more than physical (natural) beings.[218]

There are many arguments that purport to counter our logic, including assertions that a person's life before physical death has "existential" meaning (recall that we use "existential" in the sense of having meaning and purpose "in and of itself"). Yet when examined closely most of the alternative arguments are set in the time before death, within the causal sequence of events that

---

[217] Camus, Nietzsche, and Sartre all recognized the problem, acknowledge the absurdity of constructing something out of nothing, and then, not willing to see the non-physical alternative we see, proceeded to create something out of nothing, which in Nietzsche case was the Übermensch.

[218] E.O. Wilson, *The Meaning of Human Existence* (New York: W. W. Norton & Company, 2015). His views illustrate the tenuous argument for existential meaning if humanists are right, and the reason to seek alternatives.

precede death.[219] Every mainstream humanistic theory is based on the biophysics of existence before physical death. We believe that none of the arguments adequately address the period after death (perhaps with the possible exception suggested by modern physics), and therefore none adequately answer the question of how a person who no longer exists can have a past, present, or future? We recognize the seeming absurdity of the language, yet if on our death we cease to exist, then *nothing* totally consumes us.[220]

It is extremely difficult to understand that if after our physical death there is *nothing*, then there is absolutely no reason whatsoever to do anything except live our lives as if they have meaning and value. There is no rational reason to terminate our lives if *nothing* follows life. If we believe that our existence may end at physical death, then we must live for the possibility that our life may not end at physical death and/or that our physical

---

[219] Jens Johansson, "The Timing Problem," In Ben Bradley, Fred Feldman, and Jens Johansson, eds. *The Oxford Handbook of Philosophy of Death* (Oxford: Oxford University Press, 2012); Roy Sorenson, "The Symmetry Problem," In Bradley, *The Oxford Handbook of Philosophy of Death*; Jens Johansson, "Past and Future Non-existence," *The Journal of Ethics* 17 (2013): 51-64. doi:10.1007/s10892-012-9137-3; Fred Feldman, "Brueckner and Fischer on the Evil of Death," *Philosophical Studies* 162 (2013): 309-317. doi:10.1007/s11098-011-9766-6 ; John Martin Fischerand Anthony L. Brueckner, "Prenatal and Posthumous Non-existence: A Reply to Johansson," *The Journal of Ethics* 18 (2014): 1-9. doi:10.1007/s10892-013-9155-9

[220] David Hershenov, "Do Dead Bodies Pose a Problem for Biological Approaches to Personal Identity?" *Mind* 114 no. 453 (2005): 31-59. doi:10.1093/mind.fz031; Hektor Yan, "Epicurus, Death and Grammar," *Philosophia* 42 (2014): 223-242. Epicurus' (341–270 BC) embraced the philosophy that "Death does not concern us, because as long as we exist, death is not here. And when it does come, we no longer exist." His view has been widely criticized, but like Hershenov and Yen we think that the critics are missing the difference in saying that before physical death a human being experiences fear of death which is bad, and that after a physical death without existence after death there is no physical object, no physical being, who can experience anything in the past, present, or future, which might be called bad.

existence may have meaning and value even if it does end. The possibility of *nothing* absolutely frees us from any concern we may have about a physical life that has an end and demands that we live for the possibility that there is "something".

Nothing

You Can't Think About Nothing

How do we think about *nothing*? [221] The real question is *can* we think about *nothing*, can we in any way whatsoever understand or visualize *nothing*.[222] We believe that the common sense and the logical answers are the same, no, we cannot think about *nothing*. When we think about *nothing* we turn it into "something" that can be thought about. The moment we attempt to comprehend or visualize *nothing*, we interject something into *nothing*, preventing us from reaching our goal.[223]

When we define *nothing* we give it the quality of being definable, a quality that can only be given to that which is more than *nothing*. *Nothing* might be thought of as the total absence of physical reality, yet even this assigns a definition to the indefinable. The moment we think about *nothing* we make it an object that can be contemplated, we make it an object that can only be more than *nothing*.

---

[221] We are talking about absolute *nothing*, what Kuhn calls level 9 *nothing* (note that even though a Kuhn level 7 *nothing* would do for our purposes, yet we believe levels 8 and 9 are real and in some rational sense metaphysically available to us). See Robert Lawrence Kuhn, "Levels of Nothing: There Are Multiple Answers to the Question of Why the Universe Exists," *eSkeptic* 41 (2013): 50. From http://www.skeptic.com/eskeptic/13-08-28/#feature and see Robert Lawrence Kuhn, "Why This Universe? Toward a Taxonomy of Possible Explanations," *Skeptic Magazine* 13 (2007): 28. From http://www.skeptic.com/magazine/downloads/skeptic13-2_Kuhn.pdf

[222] Kuhn notes, and we agree, that an analytical philosopher would point out that it is a logical fallacy to talk about "nothing", to treat *nothing* as if it were "something" (with properties). To say "there might have been nothing" implies "it is possible that there is nothing". "There is" means "something is." So "there is nothing" means "something is nothing", which is a logical contradiction.

[223] John Leslie and Robert Lawrence Kuhn, *The Mystery of Existence: Why is There Anything at All* (Hoboken: Wiley-Blackwell, 2013); Reviewed by George FR Ellis, "The Mystery of Existence: Why is There Anything At All?" *Theology and Science* 13 (2015): 260-262. doi:10.1080/14746700.2015.1023530

We can speak of *nothing* being in an empty room. But that is not correct, for the room has dimensions and is filled with empty space. Empty space is something, an object that can be described. We can measure the volume of the room and walk through the empty space. It makes sense to walk through an empty room, it makes no sense to stroll through *nothing*.

We might say that the room itself does not exist, only the emptiness exists, therefore there is *nothing*. Yet what we are really saying is that the room does not exist within the bounded space in which we exist, which is "something". We cannot comprehend *nothing* that does not exist anywhere, anytime.

The only way we can answer the question "what is *nothing*?" is to answer it by not asking it, for if we ask the question we destroy the answer. Most people fail to recognize the fact that "something" simply cannot comprehend *nothing*. Yet what seems to be rather simple logic, that *nothing* is *nothing*, turns out to be highly contested by philosophers and scientists. Entire seminars[224] and large portions of academic careers[225] are built on *nothing*.

The prominent philosophical line of objection is that even when we say there is *nothing*, there must in fact always be something. This "*nothing* must be something" argument states that since *nothing* cannot be defined it does not exist, and therefore there can never be *nothing* and there is always something.[226] Either there is something that we are never able to

---

[224] American Museum of Natural History, Isaac Asimov Memorial Debates, "The Existence of Nothing," (2013).
(http://www.amnh.org/), https://youtu.be/1OLz6uUuMp8 Definitely worth viewing even though the panel fails to deal with *nothing*.
[225] Krauss, *A Universe from Nothing*.
[226] Parmenides said "Nor is there any void, for void is nothing, and nothing cannot be. Nor does it (what is) move, for it has no place to which it can withdraw, but is full. If there were void, it would withdraw to the void; but since there is no void, it has nowhere to withdraw to." From W.K.C. Guthrie, *A History of Greek Philosophy Volume II: The Presocratic Tradition from Parmenides to Democritus*, First published 1965. (Cambridge: Cambridge University Press, 1978), 104.

detect, or there is something that has the potential to be detected.[227] There simply is no such thing as *nothing*. This idea is often said to be *anti-nihilistic*, but we believe that view is based on semantics and a rather narrow philosophical definition of nihilism.[228]

The difficulty with the circular argument is that it is a syllogism 1) *nothing* must be something, 2) something must exist or at least may exist, therefore 3) since nothing does not and cannot exist, it has no ontological foundation. The reality is that when this logic is applied to individual physical objects it fails to describe the physical reality it claims as its metaphysical domain. Saying all that exists must be something fails to address the reality of that which does not, and perhaps never will, exist.

If it is true that unicorns do not and never will exist, then saying that a unicorn is something because it has the potential to be detected, is a semantic argument that obscures the difference in objects that may physically exist and objects that in fact never do physically exist. If we say that the pet rock we are carrying is something that exists, and then smash the rock and say that our pet rock is still something because it has the potential to be our pet rock again, then we have used semantics to avoid the intuitive difference between a pet rock and a pile of sand. If we melt Rodin's statute and remove the urn of molten bronze from the pedestal, and then are not allowed to conclude that there is

---

[227] Kevin M. Staley, "Avicenna, Aquinas and the Real Distinction: In Defense of Mere Possibilities or Why Existence Matters." *Saint Anselm Journal* 9 (2014). http://www.anselm.edu/Institutes-Centers-and-the-Arts/Institute-for-Saint-Anselm-Studies/Saint-Anselm-Journal.htm
[228] One common sense way to talk about *nothing* is to talk about something and negate it, to deny that there is something. Kuhn says that philosopher Quentin Smith might rewrite the questions like this: "There is something. But why? There might not ever have been anything at all. Why are there existents rather than no existents?" Robert Lawrence Kuhn, ed. *Closer to Truth: Science, Meaning, and the Future.* (Santa Barbara: Greenwood Publishing Group, 2007), 246. We do not agree with many conclusions that Kuhn and Smith reach, however they have a good grasp of the questions.

nothing on the pedestal, we are denied a description of the reality that Rodin's statute does not exist.

A similar but more difficult line of questions is, can something be created out of *nothing*?[229] For our purposes we will avoid the many physical and metaphysical difficulties of explaining how nothing might become something that we discussed in the chapter about cosmology.[230] In the three part causal sequence *nothing*, X exists, *nothing*, we are interested in the second two parts, X exists, *nothing*. In other words, we are interested in that which causally goes from existing to not existing.

We take the commonsense route of talking about something and negating that something (recall n-1). There is a physical human being X who exists, X experiences physical death, physical human being X does not exist. It might be said that both X and *nothing* do not exist. This approach to *nothing*, at least level 9 nothing,[231] is sufficient for our purposes. It is fully consistent with Epicurus' view that "... as long as we exist, death is not here. And when it does come, we no longer exist."

The Possibility of Nothing

We have looked at the nature of *nothing*, now we will discuss the consequences of *nothing*. The following is very hard to explain, it is by far the hardest idea we have offered and may take many readings plus a great deal of effort to understand. Even though it is similar to the philosophy of Epicurus, it is probably the closest to an original idea that we have.

It is very important for you to really understand what we are saying because if you misunderstand you might be depressed by our conclusions. If anything we say is correct it is that if what we are about to discuss is what lies in our future then there is absolutely no reason whatsoever to be depressed, anxious, fearful, or to have any other negative feelings. You must understand that fact to logically and rationally consider our conclusions.

---

[229] Dongshan, "Spontaneous Creation of the Universe from Nothing."
[230] Kuhn, "Why This Universe?"
[231] Kuhn, "Levels of Nothing."

Having spent years thinking about the consequences of *nothing*, we are not at all sure human beings can fully comprehend the possibilities. *Nothing* goes against almost every evolutionary, hereditary, environmental, and common sense logical foundation. *Nothing* is the opposite of what our minds believe to be true.

Even if you think you understand *nothing* on an intellectual level, understanding *nothing* is like understanding infinity. You may think you know what infinity is, but that confidence fades when you are faced with visualizing the physical reality of a universe that may have no beginning and no end, a universe that may have no temporal or spatial boundaries. Whether the universe is open or closed, you are faced with the disturbing task of understanding the *nothing* that lies outside the "brick wall" boundary at infinity, a boundary which does not actually exist.

We are told that what lies outside the universe is not a valid question because no answer is possible. However, simply declaring a question to be meaningless, even if that is eventually found to be true, seems unsatisfactory. Math has taught us that Y = ∞ is undefined, but that in equations a limit value for Y may be calculated as Y approaches infinity. In other words, the limit of 1 divided by x as x approaches ∞ is 0. It is never more than 1, never 0, and never less than 0. The fact that in mathematics we can approach 0 as a limit but never reach it does not undermine fundamental notions of "convergence of infinite sequences and infinite series to a well-defined limit", which is the foundation of calculus.[232] We pursue an understanding of *nothing* knowing that we can come close to, but never reach, our goal.

It takes the focus and determination of an Olympic gold medal winner to consider *nothing*. The incomprehensibility of *nothing* falsely leads to hedonism where there is no justification for it, fear where there is no logic behind the fear, depression where there is no reason to be depressed, etc. You can never reach a full understanding of *nothing,* as you approach you will

---

[232] Wikipedia. 2020. "Calculus." Last modified December 17, 2019. https://en.wikipedia.org/wiki/Calculus

engage in a Sisyphean task, always sliding back down the mountain knowing that even if you reached the summit there would be *nothing* to see. Let's take a look at the limit as we approach the unknowable.

Even though we are convinced that physical death is not the end of your existence, if it is the end should you be frightened by the certainty of your demise? If indeed you cease to exist, you need not fear death, for after your death you will feel neither pain, nor pleasure, nor peace, nor torment. "You" will no longer exist, therefore "you" will feel *nothing*. The resulting void is just that, a complete and total void.

There is *nothing* to fear, for there will be no one to experience anything negative. There is *nothing* to look forward to, for there will be no one to experience anything positive. The only way you can visualize what is usually called a "nihilistic" death is to picture yourself after death as being in the same state you were in before birth (of course you were not really in any state at all). Such a fate would not leave anything to be feared.[233]

The boundaries of human comprehension make it extremely difficult to recognize the fact that if there is a nihilistic void after physical death, then there is absolutely no reason at all to think about the *nothing* that may follow physical life. *Nothing* cannot affect our physical lives, either positively or negatively. It cannot be a part of our existence, it cannot be a part of our thoughts, it is *nothing*.

Nothing is not at the end of our life, it does not define the timeline of our memories, it does not mark the transition to another state of being or non-being. If after our physical death there is *nothing* then when we die we will not experience calm or peace or pain or distress, we will not experience anything because we will not exist. *Nothing* does not relieve us of anything simply because there will be no one to experience relief, there will be no "you" who can feel the absence of pain.

You will not remember the good times or the horrific events in your life. We need to accept the difficult but essential

---

[233] Hershenov, "Do Dead Bodies Pose a Problem for Biological Approaches to Personal Identity?"

point, if *nothing* follows physical death then there is no peaceful sleep because no one exists who can sleep, there are no nightmares because there is no one to dream. All will be as if it never was.

If you live five years in excruciating pain and there is *nothing* after physical death, then when you die the pain does not "end", it is as if those five years never happened. If you live fifty years in excruciating pain and there is *nothing* after physical death, then when you die the pain does not "end", it is as if those fifty years never happened. If there is *nothing* after physical death, you gain nothing if your physical pain lasts only five years instead of fifty years, there is no difference. In both cases on the day of your death the excruciating pain does not "end", it is as if the pain never was.

There is a profound difference between pain which ends and pain which never was. That is the key idea that is so difficult to grasp. It may seem that anything which results in pain being as if it never happened is an end to the pain we are suffering, but that is not the "reality" of not existing, of *nothing*.

Take the time to really think about the difference, hopefully you will eventually realize that if on our physical death *nothing*, then it is no worse or better if you suffer fifty years of pain or five years of pain or you never have any pain at all. If in fact there is *nothing* after physical death, then if you live one minute, or 20 or 30 or 40 or 50 more years, all the horrors in your past, present, and future will be "consumed" by *nothing*. This is not the same as saying that we find "peace" in a nihilistic death, we find *nothing*. Actually, we should not say that we "find" *nothing* after a nihilistic death, to even begin to describe the reality of *nothing* we must use the word *nothing* by itself and not say anything about it.

One of the thoughts that is entrenched in human nature and human logic is that terminating pain in life brings peace. Common sense reasoning tells us that if someone is dying of cancer, terminating that life stops the pain and brings relief to the sufferer. That makes common sense, but if there is *nothing* after physical death it is wrong. If nihilism is true and on our physical death there is *nothing*, then we are not relieved from the pain of cancer or drug use or depression or anything else, we do not exist therefore we are not relieved of anything.

If after physical death *nothing*, then all the pain of cancer or drug use or depression or anything else that we experienced during our physical life is as if it never happened. No one exists that experienced the pain, therefore no one has memories of the pain. The reality of *nothing* is that the pain is not gone, or relieved, or ended, the pain simply is not, will not be, and never was for the person who does not exist. Nihilism tells us there is no reason to seek comfort in *nothing* for it is an illusion, no matter how many years of pain are in your past, present, and future, your pain would be as if it never happened.

If there is *nothing* after physical death, there can be absolutely no benefit to a shorter life, no logical reason to want physical life to end. If there is *nothing* after death the choice to endure the most horrible pain and seek meaning and value in our life can cause us no harm. Even though human nature may make it seem absurd, if we do not exist after our physical death we have no reason to fear, or avoid, five years or fifty years of pain. The all-consuming nature of the *nothing* that may follow physical death is what human beings find almost impossible to comprehend, yet understanding the possibility of *nothing* actually frees us to live the best life we can.

The possibility of "something", non-physical life after physical death and/or existential meaning to physical life, and the freedom of *nothing* if we are wrong, leads us to the conclusion that we are free to live as long and as good a physical life as we can. If there is *nothing* after physical death then just as the past and present will be as if they never were, a future filled with joy or pain will never be. The logical imperative is that we have absolutely no reason not to live for the possibility that "something" in our life has or may have meaning and value. There is no reason not to live the most positive life we can. This is the indisputable, logical, consequence of *nothing*.

If you are living a pleasant life your initial response to the possibility of *nothing* may be that it is frightening, or if you are suffering it may feel somehow comforting, both thoughts are totally, unquestionably, wrong. If on our physical death there is *nothing*, then there is no rational or logical reason to think about physical death as fearful or peaceful. If there is *nothing* after physical death then the experience of physical death (perhaps it is better to say the experience that never happens) is the same if it occurs in one day or one year or one hundred years, during a period of great joy or great pain. There would be *nothing* in your future to look forward to, there would be *nothing* in your future to fear.

If you really understand what this means, you recognize that the possibility of *nothing* allows us to endure all of the physical and emotional pain we experience no matter how horrific, and to live the most positive life we can with the hope that there is existential meaning in our physical life and/or that there is a non-physical life after our death. The possibility of *nothing* gives you the strength to work through pain, so that you may search for a reason for living, and live for the real and permanent possibilities life may offer. We can choose to live as positive a life as we possibly can, knowing that if life has meaning and purpose we are doing all that we can to live a good life which is not rendered meaningless by physical death, and that if in fact there is *nothing* after death all the physical and emotional pain will be as if it never was. The possibility of meaning and purpose in our daily lives, no matter how slight we may believe it to be, and the freedom of *nothing* if we are wrong, is all that is required for us to live the best life we can.

If there is *nothing* after death, then it makes no difference to you if your life was filled with pain or pleasure, because you will not exist to feel pain or pleasure. If we are to be honest with ourselves, the logical conclusion is that since we cannot scientifically prove that which is beyond human ability to observe, Occam's razor favors existence after death as the most likely place to find meaning and value in life. If there is an existence after death, then by having chosen to endure physical pain and chosen to live the most positive physical life you can, you may find that after your physical death memories of even the worst pain are overwhelmed by "joy" and "disappear". If there is an existence after physical death (or based on what science tells us about the physical universe, the much less likely idea that there is some other existential meaning to life), then enduring a lifetime of pain and emotional hurt may result in a timeless eternity of peace and happiness. If there is an existence after death, and you do not choose to live the most positive life you can, then you may be rejecting eternal peace and happiness.

Alternatives to the Possibility of *Nothing*

What should our response be to all of this? We strongly believe that there is absolutely no reason not to live for the possibility that life has meaning and value. We think we are right about the transitory nature of physical / natural consciousness, but we may be totally wrong. If we are wrong, if each of us has a singular physical / natural consciousness that somehow survives physical death, or if there is some other form of existential existence that gives meaning and purpose to our physical lives, then our life may have meaning and value even if there is no non-physical life after death. We will briefly consider some of the possibilities, as you read further you should remember that they may or may not reflect reality. We will also look at the possibility we are living in an atemporal universe.

Reincarnation, Fact or Fiction?

There are a significant number of religions that believe a soul, a form of consciousness, survives physical death and remains in the physical world. The best-known idea is that of reincarnation, where the essence of a human being is reborn into another physical being. This is the belief of many who practice Indian religions,[234] Spiritism, Theosophy, Eckankar, and among the Kabbalah, Druze, and Rosicrucians sects.[235] Buddhism is more complex, Tibetian Buddhists believe in something which might be called never ending rebirth.[236] For other Buddhists reincarnation leads to a state of nirvana, ultimate peace, which is somewhat different to continuing rebirths. The basic concept is the same,

---

[234] A classic 1926 introduction to Indian religions is by Ramchandra Dattatraya Ranade, "A Constructive Survey of Upanishadic Philosophy, Being a Systematic Introduction to Indian Metaphysics." https://archive.org/details/A.Constructive.Survey.of.Upanishadic.Phil osophy.by.R.D.Ranade.1926.djvu

[235] Anil Kumar Mysore Nagaraj, Raveesh Bevinahalli Nanjegowda, and S. M. Purushothama. "The Mystery of Reincarnation." *Indian Journal of Psychiatry* 55 supp. 2 (2013): S171. doi:10.4103/0019-5545.105519

[236] The 14th Dalai Lama. "Reincarnation," (2011). http://www.dalailama.com/messages/statement-of-his-holiness-the-fourteenth-dalai-lama-tenzin-gyatso-on-the-issue-of-his-reincarnation

individual human consciousness is believed to occupy a succession of physical entities.

In rebirth consciousness is said not to be a simple transfer from one human being to the next. Most scholars of the religions that believe in reincarnation explain it as being like a candle flame being passed from one candle to the next, the old flame and the new flame are not the same but there is continuity. Most who believe in reincarnation do so as a matter of faith, either the result of having grown up in or having adopted a particular religion that teaches some form of rebirth. There is no question that millions of people sincerely believe that in some sense they have existed in the past and will continue to exist in the future in the physical universe.

What do scientists have to say? The most quoted expert is Ian Stevenson, a researcher who dedicated his life to objectively documenting reincarnation.[237] Stevenson (1918-2007) was the founder (in 1967) and director of the Division of Perceptual Studies in the Psychiatry and Neuro-behavioral Sciences department of the University of Virginia's Health System. Research continues at the University of Virginia, with case studies being compiled based on interviews with children and families. Many believe that memories of past lives are most vivid during the first few years of a new life, and then fade due to the child becoming more engaged with his or her present life. It is fair to say that a number of respected doctors and scientists believe that patients have recounted to them memories that they acquired during a past physical life.

Should we embrace Dr. Stevenson and his colleague's findings? You will need to read the materials for yourself, but we can say that after doing so we are not convinced. While it appears that Dr. Stevenson was sincere and honest, his enthusiasm for the idea of reincarnation seems to have colored his judgment. There are a few cases he documents which, if the statements recorded are completely factual, would represent moderate support for

---

[237] Ian Stevenson, *Children Who Remember Previous Lives: A Question of Reincarnation*, Revised edition. (Jefferson NC: McFarland, 2000).

reincarnation.[238] But those cases are only a few out of the 3,000+ he compiled.

When we first read Dr. Stevenson's and his successors' books and articles, we were at least tentatively convinced that they represented evidence of reincarnation. It was only after carefully reading the texts, and studying the circumstances, that the foundation weakened. For example, Stevenson thought one of the strongest cases was of a 5-year-old Lebanese-Druse boy named Imad Elawar who he interviewed in 1964.

Stevenson recorded the Elwar family's statements in support of Imad's belief that he lived a previous life in a nearby village, and he traveled with them to that village trying to verify the story. After some significant reinterpretation, he believed that 80% of the boy's statements were verified. Later reviewers reduced that number to perhaps 63%, but to us even that figure seems hard to support.[239] When you look at the list of statements determined by the researchers to be verified facts, many seem so broad as to be useless. We do not believe that there is sufficient evidence to rule out the recollections of Imad having been fitted to the facts as they were recounted by his parents and translators. Interestingly it appears that no follow-up interview of Imad was ever done by Stevenson or his colleagues when he grew older.[240]

In another study Stevenson's seemingly objective comparison of birthmarks in both past and current lives is, on second look, difficult to have confidence in. For example,

---

[238] Ian Stevenson, "Birthmarks and Birth Defects Corresponding to Wounds on Deceased Persons," *Journal of Scientific Exploration* 7 no. 4 (1993): 403-416.
http://www.medicine.virginia.edu/clinical/departments/psychiatry/sections/cspp/dops/dr.-stevensons-publications/STE39stevenson-1.pdf
[239] Julio Cesar de Siqueira Barros, "Another Look at the Imad Elawar Case - A Review of Leonard Angel's Critique of This 'Past Life Memory Case Study'" (2004).We read this review carefully many times and still found it inconclusive.
http://www.criticandokardec.com.br/imad_elawar_revisited.html
[240] As of the date of publication of our book Imad would be in his mid-50's.

Stevenson includes a woman who said she was murdered in her past life by a shotgun blast to the chest.[241] He affirmed her story based on two round birthmarks which he concluded were suggestive of small and large buckshot. The immediate question is why would two small birthmarks correspond to the damage done by a shotgun?

He also discusses a man with a light pigmented area on his chest who stated he was killed in his past life by a shotgun blast fired at close range. Again, this seems a stretch, especially when there was no exit pigmentation on his back. Nine out of 44 cases exhibited birthmarks which with a bit of imagination might suggest entry and/or exit wounds, but to us the source of the marks seems unresolved. In most cases the person claiming to have lived a past life resided in a country where reincarnation was accepted as true, self-reported the individual who he or she was in the previous life, and could have constructed the events for numerous sociologic and psychologic reasons.

For example, some 3000 BCE the Hindu teacher Maharishi Parasara described the meaning of moles and birthmarks. The parents of a Hindu child would want to explain away the existence of birthmarks that had negative meanings and affirm the proclaimed implications of positive marks. In general, light pigmented birthmarks are positive, dark ones negative, but position on the body can change that interpretation. Stevenson suggested that parents would not want to associate their children with a previous life in the same caste or a lower caste, or with someone who had an unsavory history. While some parents recounted negative associations, in fact many of the children reported memories of life in a higher caste which would presumably be a positive social claim for the parents. Even those who remembered life as a criminal gained notoriety and a certain degree of respect from other believers simply for having remembered a past life.

In his preface to the 1974 second edition, Stevenson himself said "Neither any case individually nor all of them

---

[241] Stevenson, "Birthmarks and Birth Defects".

collectively offers anything like a proof of reincarnation."[242] This is a very strong statement by the researcher. A careful review by a third party concluded "If I were to answer the question 'Is there empirical evidence for reincarnation?' presently my answer would be: 'The evidence is weak. But it is certainly there.'" Our review leads us to conclude that the evidence is suggestive but weak, not verifiable, and not without reasonable alternate explanations. What we have from respected researchers with open minds is a few dozen cases deemed at best as some evidence, but not strong or conclusive evidence.

For those looking for proof of reincarnation, Stevenson's work is proof that they are right. For those looking for proof that there is no reincarnation, Stevenson's work is proof that they are right.[243] For us Stevenson's work is interesting, but not sufficient to base any conclusions on.

The intuitive question is why, after fifty years of intense effort by researchers, is there no solid evidence proving or disproving reincarnation? Tens of millions of people believe in reincarnation and recite facts about their past lives. It is difficult to believe that not one of these cases has produced hard facts without the need for interpretation and manipulation of data. Based on the objective evidence our intuitive belief is that reincarnation does not offer a significant possibility of meaningful permanent consciousness.

Near Death Experiences (NDE)

Agreeing that physical consciousness ends at physical death is not the same as saying that consciousness ends at physical death. Many human beings have a strong intuitive belief that non-physical consciousness exists after physical death. Some patients describe strikingly similar experiences during the period

---

[242] Ian Stevenson, *Twenty Cases Suggestive of Reincarnation* (Charlottesville: University of Virginia Press, 1980).
[243] Even if reincarnation is real we face the practical problem that when the universe becomes a hostile environment for biophysical beings there will be no longer be any physical bodies in which to be reincarnated.

after the onset of cardiac arrest and before resuscitation.[244] Reports of near-death experiences (NDE's) are anecdotally well documented,[245] yet objective scientific evidence is lacking for both the nature of the experiences and possible physical causes.[246]

Perhaps the most scientifically rigorous attempt to provide evidence of cognitive / mental experiences and awareness during cardiac arrest, when the brain is presumed to be unconscious, was the AWARE study.[247] It was a four year multi-center observational study, utilizing a three stage quantitative and qualitative interview, which reported results in 2014. The results were typical of studies trying to document the amorphous nature of consciousness, out of 2060 cardiac arrests 140 survivors completed stage 1 interviews. 101 of those completed stage 2 interviews with 46% having memories of events and 9% having defined NDE's.

Only 2 of the 101 patients reported a potentially verifiable period of conscious awareness of surroundings during the time cerebral function was not expected (only one was well enough to complete the stage 3 interview). The best scientific study to date

---

[244] Gideon Lichfield, "The Science of Near-Death Experiences Empirically Investigating Brushes With the Afterlife." *The Atlantic*, (April 2015l). http://www.theatlantic.com/features/archive/2015/03/the-science-of-near-death-experiences/386231/; Dossey, Larry, "Nonlocal Mind: A (Fairly) Brief History of the Term," *EXPLORE: The Journal of Science and Healing* (2014). doi:10.1016/j.explore.2014.12.001

[245] Janice Minor Holden, Bruce Greyson, and Debbie James, eds. *The Handbook of Near-Death Experiences: Thirty Years of Investigation* (Santa Barbara: Praeger/ABC-CLIO, 2009).

[246] Adriana Sleutjes, Alexander Moreira-Almeida, and Bruce Greyson, "Almost 40 Years Investigating Near-Death Experiences: An Overview of Mainstream Scientific Journals," *The Journal of Nervous and Mental Disease* 202 (2014): 833-836. doi:10.1097/NMD.0000000000002050000205

[247] Sam Parnia, Ken Spearpoint, Gabriele de Vos, Peter Fenwick, Diana Goldberg, Jie Yang, Jiawen Zhu et al. "AWARE-AWAreness During Resuscitation-A Prospective Study," *Resuscitation* 85 no. 12 (2014): 1799-1805. doi:10.1016/j.resuscitation.2014.09.004

came up with one patient out of 2060 cardiac arrests who appears to have accurately described his resuscitation during a period when current theories say he should not have been conscious of the event.

What should we make of the AWARE study? It is clear that scientific study of NDE's is very difficult. The researchers had installed 1000 shelves near hospital ceilings, in areas where cardiac resuscitation normally occurs, with images visible only to someone looking down from above. The idea was that if anyone reported watching their own resuscitation from the ceiling as many NDE survivors do, they should also be able to recall the test image. The one person reporting his resuscitation did so from the vantage point of a ceiling corner, but he was in a room that did not have a shelf. Aware leaves us with evidence that believers would perhaps welcome as promising, but that skeptics and objective scientists would call incomplete and inconclusive.

What about the rest of the literature? Dr. Eben Alexander is one of the best-known people who state that they have been in heaven.[248] His journey occurred during a week when he was in a coma due to bacterial meningitis. His account has been given weight due to his reputation as a surgeon, however Esquire magazine later published an article calling him a charlatan.[249] NDE supporters rallied to Dr. Alexander' defense, skeptics said it was just another case like a boy who through his father's book vividly claimed he went to heaven, only to later recant his story.[250]

---

[248] Eben Alexander, *Proof of Heaven Deluxe Edition with DVD: A Neurosurgeon's Journey Into the Afterlife* (New York: Simon and Schuster, 2013).

[249] Luke Dittrich, "The Prophet," *Esquire* (July 2013). http://www.esquire.com/entertainment/interviews/a23248/the-prophet/

[250] Sarah Eekhoff Zylstra, "The 'Boy Who Came Back from Heaven' Retracts Story", *Christianity Today* (2015, January). http://www.christianitytoday.com/gleanings/2015/january/boy-who-came-back-from-heaven-retraction.html

Dr. Larry Dossey has a strongly held opinion of the mechanisms behind NDE's.[251] He believes that quantum non-locality is not only correct, but that all conscious beings are part of a collective consciousness that is both everywhere and eternal. That consciousness may be called the mind and may act through the physical brain, but it is actually something that exists beyond individuals. He takes the concept of non-locality in physics to its extreme and jumps to a universal non-physical consciousness that controls the physical.[252]

His view may be right, physical consciousness may be a projection of a non-physical pantheistic consciousness, but his conclusions represent leaps that are not necessary to understanding individual consciousness. What is more troubling is his failure to explain how an individual human consciousness would retain self-awareness when merged with a collective consciousness. We are not told how a universal consciousness could preserve individual minds and meaningful existence. We don't believe Dossey has established a scientific, or even an intuitive, foundation for his beliefs.

Dr. Pim van Lommelis has spent some twenty years studying NDE's and is the author of many articles discussing the mind / brain mystery. He concludes that the evidence is strong enough to believe that the mind exists apart from the physical brain, and acts through it during physical life. "For this reason we indeed should seriously consider the possibility that death, like birth, can only be a transition to another state of consciousness, and that during life the body functions as an interface or place of resonance."[253] Like other physicians exploring the matter he thinks we need to pursue quality scientific research to see how much we can discover about the "non-local" mind.

---

[251] Larry Dossey, "Something Higher," Forthcoming. *Explore: The Journal of Science and Healing* (2015).
doi:10.1016/j.explore.2015.04.011
[252] Dossey, "Nonlocal Mind – A Fairly Brief History".
[253] Pim van Lommel, "Non-local Consciousness A Concept Based on Scientific Research on Near-Death Experiences During Cardiac Arrest," *Journal of Consciousness Studies* 20 (2013): 7-48.
doi:10.1080/02604020500412808

NDE's may be glimpses of existence after physical death, or they may be part of the process of the body and brain shutting down. There are reasonable arguments supporting both possibilities. Based on our review of the literature we do not think there is sufficient information to determine which explanation is true. Our limited understanding of NDE's does not add evidence needed to help us choose which of our three classifications of consciousness is most likely to represent reality. We do not believe that NDE's and other reports of conscious experiences offer objective, scientific, evidence of a significant individual physical conscious existence after physical death.

Existential Meaning

There is a third possibility that the intuitive feeling human beings have that their physical past cannot change or be lost is based on some real, yet unknown, physical or natural model of our universe. As we have said, virtually everyone is certain that if they are eleven years old they have already experienced their tenth year of life, and that nothing can take from them the past experience of being ten years old. The intuitive feeling is very strong that our physical life makes a positive or negative contribution to human existence, and that our physical life is a permanent part of the physical universe. We need to look at what science, and philosophy based on that science, have to say before addressing existentialism as it is usually understood.

Block Universe

What does physics have to say about all this? To see why we do not believe that science or philosophy provide us with a physical / natural past that preserves human consciousness, we need to look at two interpretations of cosmologic theories, the block universe and atemporal models, and one other metaphysical possibility, existentialism. There are many variations, but the three we discuss illustrate the most important viewpoints. The more promising, and mysterious, questions about the permanence of physical existence are found in the physics of relativity. We need to recognize that the very difficult conclusions that we reach about existence are not necessarily supported by conventional interpretations of general relativity and quantum mechanics. The understandings that human beings have of the physical universe and existence are fundamentally incomplete, we cannot reach objective, definitive, scientific conclusions about existence and consciousness based on current knowledge.

Early concepts of Newtonian space and time as absolute metaphysical entities, and other models where time flows from past to present to future, would seem to be fully consistent with our conclusions about finite physical (natural) existence. However, modern physics tells us that the universe is much more complex than it was once thought to be. At the start of the third millennium, it is generally accepted that we exist in some kind of four dimensional "space-time".[254] The mathematician Hermann Minkowski, who helped formalize the math of space-time, said "...henceforth, space by itself, and time by itself, have vanished into the merest shadows and only a kind of blend of the two exists in its own right."[255]

The first possibility we will look at is based on the fact that most interpretations suggest that the physical existence of each

---

[254] See our website http://www.ws5.com/spacetime

[255] Gregory L Nager, *The Geometry of Makowskis spacetime: An Introduction to the Mathematics of the Special Theory of Relativity* (New York: Springer Science & Business Media, 2012); Vesselin Petkov, ed. *Minkowski Spacetime: A Hundred Years Later,* (New York: Springer, 2010).

human being somehow persists in a block universe as a permanent collection of events on the individual's worldline. Space-time is essentially the history of the entire universe, containing every "event" that ever happens.[256] A "worldline" is the history of an observer in "space-time". Each point on the worldline of a human being is generally thought to be a real physical event[257] that represents a unique sequential moment in the life of that individual, from birth to death. Conventional wisdom is that the worldline of a human being is the complete lifetime of the human being, so that human life is in some real sense a permanent part of space-time.[258] If this is so, perhaps we have a permanent physical past that is etched in the fabric of space-time.

The best way to understand a block model is to think of motion picture photographed on film (young readers who have grown up on digital videos may need to read about how film works). When we watch a movie recorded on film we see people walking and talking. If we examine each frame of the film all that we see is still pictures, there is no motion at all. In a block universe each frame of the film represents a single slice of the block universe (known as a plane of simultaneity).

We see motion only when we start the projector and view the frames of film, slices of the block universe, as a rapidly displayed sequence of images and events. In fact, nothing is moving in any of the individual frames of film, or any of the slices of universe. If we examine the entire reel of film or the entire block universe we see no motion at all. No matter how we conceptualize this idea, motion is an illusion.

---

[256] Michael Friedman, *Foundations of Space-Time Theories: Relativistic Physics and Philosophy of Science,* First printing 1983. (Princeton NJ: Princeton University Press, 2014).

[257] Mauro Dorato, "Substantivalism, Relationism, and Structural Spacetime Realism." *Foundations of Physics* 30 (2000): 1605-1628. doi:10.1023/A:1026442015519

[258] Mauro Dorato, "The Alexandroff Present and Minkowski Spacetime: Why it Cannot Do What it has Been Asked to Do." In The *Philosophy of Science in a European Perspective* (Amsterdam: Springer Netherlands, 2011).

Two variations of the block model, neither of which seem compatible with relativity, are the expanding block and the evolving block. The expanding block model is a movie that is still being photographed, so that what has been filmed is fixed and unchanging while the remaining scenes in the movie are still a work in progress. An evolving block model is a completed film that is shown only once in a movie theater, from beginning to end.

Worldlines

Explanations by physicists intended for a public audience often say that an object is the entire worldline of that object, or that a human being is his or her worldline, but they do not really explain what is meant by this. However, scientists almost universally conclude that each event in a human being's life exists as an event in space-time,[259] so that if we could observe the point on a worldline that is the tenth birthday of someone who is now twenty years old, we would see that person experiencing their tenth birthday. We would not see a copy, or a repeat, of the particular day, we would see the person's tenth birthday as it is occurring, period!

The theory of relativity tells us that all of the laws of physics are the same for every inertial observer. If we live in a fully relational, relativistic universe, we simply cannot prefer observations made in the inertial frame of reference of one observer over observations made in the inertial frame of reference of any other observer, no matter where they may be located in space-time. An apparent consequence of this fact is that for one observer your tenth birthday occurs before your eleventh birthday, while for another (spatially separated) observer your eleventh birthday occurs before your tenth! Relativity tells us that both observers are 100% correct in their observations (this is one of many reasons we prefer an atemporal model of our physical universe). The cosmos is a very strange place indeed!

Classic interpretations imply that each individual exists as discrete human consciousness in the billions of discrete events

---

[259] Dieks, *The Ontology of Spacetime.*

located at every point[260] along that individual's worldline. Some physicists describe this by saying that there are many "now's"; others say there are billions of approximate isomorphs of "me"; many claim there are billions of other worlds in which various versions of "me" co-exist; etc. It seems reasonable to conclude that modern physics tells us that if we live in a block universe, literally billions of discrete, very real, versions of each of us occupy space-time!

So how do we account for the inevitable progression from birth to death? In the 5th appendix of the 15th edition of his book on relativity Einstein wrote "Since there exists in this four dimensional structure no longer any sections which represent now objectively, the concepts of happening and becoming are indeed not completely suspended, but yet complicated."[261] What did he mean, "...happening and becoming are indeed not completely suspended"?

Was this consistent with his statement when he consoled the widow of a friend, saying that although her husband had preceded her in death it was of no consequence, "...for us physicists believe the separation between past, present, and future is only an illusion, although a convincing one."[262] Yet he also said "A photograph never grows old. You and I change, people change all through the months and years but a photograph always remains the same. How nice to look at a photograph of mother or father taken many years ago. You see them as you remember them. But as people live on, they change completely. That is why I think a photograph can be kind."[263]

---

[260] Craig Callender and Nick Huggett, eds. *Physics Meets Philosophy at the Planck Scale: Contemporary Theories in Quantum Gravity* (Cambridge: Cambridge Univ. Press, 2001); Vesselin Petkov, "Time and Reality of Worldtubes," arXiv preprint arXiv:0812.0355 (2008). http://arxiv.org/pdf/0812.0355.pdf

[261] Albert Einstein, *Relativity: The Special and General Theory*. Reprint. (London: Routledge, 2001), 108.

[262] Polkinghorne, John Charlton, *Theology in the Context of Science* (New Haven: Yale University Press, 2009): 58

[263] Alan Windsor Richards, *Einstein as I Knew Him* (Princeton, NJ: Harvest House Press, 1979).

It is clear that Einstein believed that the past, present, and future coexist, yet he also realized that in some unexplained manner happening and becoming occur, "But as people live on, they change completely." There is no answer to what being and becoming means in a block universe, and only a rather unsatisfactory tentative answer for an expanding / evolving block universe.

Furthermore, if we live in some kind of block universe we must face the fact that approximate isomorphs of "me" exist at every event along my worldline. Each frame of the film is an independent still photo of the actors at a single point in the movie. If the same actor appears in all the scenes, he or she is the human being we see in every frame of the film. There is no rational way to point to one frame and say this is the real actor and the others are imposters.

If you think of the reel of film as your worldline in space-time, and each frame as a single event on that worldline, you can see why the block universe does not help us understand consciousness. Like the actor in the film, a lifetime of totally isolated "you's" exist at each point on your worldline, only one of which is the conscious you reading this paragraph.

Now that you have moved on to this next paragraph even the you reading the last sentence is but one of the billions of you's on your worldline. There is no sense of a single you that is a conscious human being with a permanent existence. The block universe in any form does not allow for a unique conscious human being who exists at a single point in the past, present, or future.

It would seem that this characteristic of all popular space-time theories leaves us without tools for building a rational model of a universe that contains a conscious worldline that is the "me" reading this book. Rather it tells us that there is, and always will be, a set of unique "me's" that somehow exist in space-time at every single event on my worldline. Me on my tenth, twentieth, thirtieth birthdays and all the days in-between. We might want to say that we are the sum of all the points, yet the assertion that a human being is his or her entire worldline, from birth to death, does not appear to be consistent with the general consensus that every event along a worldline has a singular existence that cannot be preferred over any other event on that worldline.

Many Worlds

The many-worlds (multiverse) theory we mentioned before is one possible explanation of how every event might be fixed and unchanging, and at the same time could have a different outcome based on quantum probabilities. It states that every time an event occurs which has a possible required alternative, the universe splits into two identical parts. In one part one alternative occurs and in the other part the other alternative occurs, so that all possibilities are realized. This may seem like science fiction, yet surveys of theoretical physicists and cosmologists confirm that many, or even most depending on their areas of expertise, believe we must adopt some form of many-worlds, many-minds, multiple existence, theory.[264] Remember, this is current accepted thought, and not just speculative ideas.

In a block universe or in an infinite number of parallel universes there is no singular physical "you" who survives physical / natural death. If the scientists are correct, it would seem to be impossible to find meaning and value for a singular you in the collective existence of each of the billions of instances of individual consciousness, no single one of which is the you who can live a meaningful life. All of the popular interpretations of relativistic and quantum theories lead us to the same conclusion, if you do not have a singular permanent existence, your life has no meaning and your choices make no difference to you, simply because there is no single physical "you" who exists before or after physical death (please remember, we believe that life has meaning and value).

---

[264] Max Tegmark, "The Interpretation of Quantum Mechanics: Many Worlds or Many Words?" arXiv preprint (1997). http://arxiv.org/pdf/quant-ph/9709032.pdf

Time

Are there other interpretations of general relativity and quantum mechanics that help identify a singular you? If so, do these favor a permanent physical you or do they support our conclusions about physical / natural consciousness?

The second possible interpretation, the one that we favor over the classical block universe model, brings into question the very nature of space-time. At initial glance, the concept of a permanent physical space-time, a block universe, seems to imply that human beings have a permanent physical past, present, and future. Most people assume that the math of space-time describes a permanent physical reality that surrounds us, a very real, very physical, space-time in which we exist.[265] This may or may not be the case.

The limited number of physicists who understand the incredibly difficult math, realize that the theory of general relativity tells us that the universe may be completely described without using a fundamental temporal variable, without even defining what we call "time". The time we measure on a stopwatch that we use to clock a foot race is derived from comparing the motion of the runner from the starting line to the finish line with the motion of the hand rotating around the face of the watch. The time on the stopwatch may not be, as Newton thought, a fundamental quantity in nature.

Rather it may be nothing more than a comparison of the motion of the person running down the track relative to the motion of the hands of the stopwatch. Therefore, we may be justified in concluding that time is derived from relative motion, but that relative motion does not require the passage of time. It may be true that fundamental time simply does not exist.[266]

---

[265] In special and general relativity simultaneity is relative but locality is absolute. Giovanni Amelino-Camelia, Laurent Freidel, Jerzy Kowalski-Glikman, and Lee Smolin. "Relative Locality: A Deepening of the Relativity Principle," *International Journal of Modern Physics D* 20 (2011): 2867-2873. doi:10.1142/S0218271811020743
[266] Carlo Rovelli, "Forget Time."

This is a shocking idea for human beings who are confronted with the ticking away of years, days, hours, and seconds. Yet if you think about it, a year is nothing more than the relative motion of the earth going around the sun, a day is the relative motion of the earth rotating around its axis, an hour is a fraction of the motion we call a day measured by a quartz "moving" in a watch, a second is very close to the relative motion of a beating heart. We don't expect to convince you in a few paragraphs that time is an illusion, it took years of reading and thought for us to reach that conclusion, but we do want you to recognize that there is a strong possibility that fundamental time does not exist. If this is a correct interpretation of general relativity, it can lead to the conclusion that there is no fundamental (not derived) temporality of any kind associated with our universe.

There are serious objections to this line of thought.[267] In its most popular forms, the other 20th century revolution in physics, quantum mechanics, incorporates a fundamental temporal variable. Some scientists believe that general relativity will be found to be incomplete, and that quantum mechanics tells us that time does in fact exist.[268] Other physicists agree that the universe lacks a fundamental temporal variable by which the universe evolves, yet they also believe that in some very real sense the universe exhibits fundamental temporality.[269]

Atemporal Universe

None-the-less, there are a few respected physicists who believe that we should accept what general relativity is telling us, that there is no fundamental temporal variable in the universe, and find a way to modify quantum mechanics to eliminate both

---

[267] Lee Smolin, *Time Reborn: From the Crisis in Physics to the Future of the Universe* (New York: Houghton Mifflin Harcourt, 2013). Smolin's theory is more radical than the idea of atemporality which we favor because he postulates that the laws of physics evolve.
[268] Craig Callender, ed. *The Oxford Handbook of Philosophy of Time* (Oxford: Oxford University Press, 2011).
[269] Nick Huggett, "Skeptical Notes on a Physics of Passage," *Annals of the New York Academy of Sciences* 1326 (2014): 9-17. doi:10.1111/nyas.12514

time and temporality from quantum theory. Given the success of general relativity in predicting experimental results, we believe that this is the correct approach.[270] We are convinced that if and when physicists discover a broad model that incorporates both relativity and quantum theories, what is usually called a theory of quantum gravity, it will not have any kind of fundamental temporal variable associated with it, and we will find that the universe is fundamentally atemporal in nature.[271]

In an atemporal universe we are actors on a stage where time does not exist until[272] something moves. Every actor and prop that moves does so as a result of a causal sequence, not because of the passage of time. For a table and chair on the stage, there is no relative motion, no passage of time.[273] It is only when an actor pushes a cart across the stage that time happens. The motion creates the emergent time.

Memories of rehearsing the play are not things of the past, but rather are mental images that reside in the brain of the actor standing on the stage. Memories are timeless scripts embedded in actors minds as they perform the scene. Each event in the causal chain causes the next event which causes the next, each event (scene) ceases to exist as it triggers the next.

---

[270] Abhay Ashtekar, Beverly K. Berger, James Isenberg, and Malcolm AH MacCallum, "General Relativity and Gravitation: A Centennial Perspective." *arXiv preprint arXiv:1409.5823* (2014). http://arxiv.org/pdf/1409.5823v1.pdf

[271] Julian Barbour, Tim Koslowski, and Flavio Mercati, "The Solution to the Problem of Time in Shape Dynamics," *Classical and Quantum Gravity* 31, no. 15 (2014): 155001. [preprint http://arxiv.org/pdf/1302.6264.pdf] We need to recognize Barbour as one of the early supporters of atemporal theory. He now champions a radically different zero-dimensional temporal variable, however we are not ready to accept his shape dynamics model.

[272] We use tensed language to describe the progression of causal, not temporal, events.

[273] The actor and the cart experience temporality, perhaps the chair and table that do not move relative to each other remain atemporal in their "domain"?

If the theory of general relativity is in fact part of the illusive theory of quantum gravity, and if we do in fact live in an atemporal universe, then it is indeed quite possible that physical events in our lives either exist or do not exist. The statement that a point on a worldline exists in the universe may be false, true, false, with no sense that false is "before" or "after" true! If so, then it may be quite literally true that your tenth birthday does not exist, does exist, does not exist in the universe.[274]

Perhaps you believe that your tenth birthday is a permanent part of your past only because it is part of your current memories, not because it exists in some kind of permanent physical space-time. Note that our view is what most philosophers call "extreme presentism", other more sympathetic philosophers call it a form of "existence presentism". At the start of the third millennium our view has been rejected, or at least strongly criticized, by most scientists. Yet a growing number of physicists recognize that to make sense of reality we must adopt a new framework, one which may very well be atemporal, and perhaps aspatial[275] (relative position and causation matter, not spatial / temporal measurements between events). [276]

If we live in an essentially atemporal universe, there is state evolution but no time (in some of our other publications we discuss similarities and differences between atemporal and block universe models).[277] If there is no non-physical existence after death, then we believe that in an atemporal world physical / natural death consumes each human being's past, present, and future. This is very difficult to understand and accept, yet the idea

---

[274] Even though they might not agree, we believe our view is consistent with the work of Rovelli, Tallent, and Cramer.

[275] "Spacetime—a creation of well-known actors?" *PhysOrg*, (November 9, 2018). https://phys.org/news/2018-11-spacetimea-creation-well-known-actors.htm.

[276] Kevin H. Knutha and Bahreyni, Newshaw. "A Potential Foundation for Emergent Spacetime," *J. Math. Phys.* 55, 112501 (2014). https://doi.org/10.1063/1.4899081, Retrieved from https://aip.scitation.org/doi/full/10.1063/1.4899081.

[277] See links to references and our general discussion on our website http://www.ws5.com/spacetime

that there is no fundamental temporality, and that this fact leads to the annihilation of our physical past, appears to us to be the correct interpretation of our physical universe. Remember that our conclusions are based on very complex and controversial relativistic and quantum science, we think we are right but we may be wrong.

The reason that we cannot be more certain that our conclusions are correct is simply because no one knows what physics will look like if and when relativity and quantum theories are united. Furthermore, there is no way to tell how long it will take to find answers to the basic questions raised by modern physics. Indeed, it is quite possible that we will never know the answers to many of our most fundamental questions. We believe that the universe is essentially atemporal,[278] and that physical death annihilates our physical / natural[279] (but not any non-physical)[280] past, present, and future, but we may simply be wrong.

Atemporal Quantum Probabilities

How do we reconcile the block universe space-time of general relativity with the uncertain future of quantum probabilities? Can quantum mechanics be understood from a different perspective? We will briefly discuss John Cramer's Transactional Interpretation (TI) of quantum theory theory as a simplified overview of deBroglie pilot waves.[281]

---

[278] Spacetime, quantum gravity, and cosmology are fascinating topics, we highly recommend that readers make a conscious effort to stay current with future developments – current reliable sources include http://www.nature.com/nphys/index.html, http://www.physics.org/news.asp, http://physicsworld.com, and http://www.scientificamerican.com/physics/.

[279] Our classifications (1) Physical Consciousness – Dependent and (2) Physical / Natural Consciousness – Independent.

[280] Our classification (3) Non-Physical Consciousness – Independent.

[281] Natalie Wolchover, "Famous Experiment Dooms Alternative to Quantum Weirdness," *Quanta Magazine*, October 11, 2018. https://www.quantamagazine.org/famous-experiment-dooms-pilot-wave-alternative-to-quantum-weirdness-20181011/

The most popular quantum theory,[282] the Copenhagen Interpretation, states that there is no physical nature to quantum probabilities until observation triggers collapse of the wave function. The waves themselves are essentially mathematical constructs and do not represent reality. Cramer, a teaching physicist and prolific science fiction writer, proposed that non-locality is grounded in an atemporal understanding of quantum mechanical wave functions as real waves physically present in space rather than as mathematical representations of knowledge.

Cramer introduced advanced and retarded waves which allow for exchange of a single quantum of energy, momentum, etc., between a present emitter and a single future absorber, all through the medium of a transaction. Cramer based his idea on a Wheeler-Feynman exchange of advanced and retarded waves, a time-symmetric interaction of a retarded field which propagates into the future and an advanced field which propagates into the past.

If you think about an ocean wave striking a beachfront concrete barrier you can visualize the wave crashing into the concrete as the "retarded wave", and the bounce back in the opposite direction as the "advanced wave". The bounce back, advanced wave, literally dampens the ocean wave that is crashing into the barrier. The retarded and advanced waves, future and past waves, keep interacting until the transaction is completed with a "handshake" across space-time, essentially until a form of equilibrium is reached. This completion of the transaction is what selects a specific position and momentum from among the quantum possibilities, not observation of the process. The key point is that atemporal interactions of the advanced and retarded waves produce no present event until the transaction is completed.

[282] Maximilian Schlosshauer, Johannes Kofler, and Anton Zeilinger, "A Snapshot of Foundational Attitudes Toward Quantum Mechanics," (2013). doi:10.1016/j.shpsb.2013.04.004 [preprint http://arxiv.org/abs/1301.1069]

TI has been floating around for almost 30 years,[283] however zero percent of physicists surveyed in 2013 picked it when asked what their favorite interpretation of quantum mechanics was.[284] Despite the lack of popularity, Cramer's atemporal waves suggest one approach to demystifying quantum theory. If you will recall our discussion of the block universe and time, you may see a possible link between Carlo Rovelli's view of the universe[285] and Cramer's TI. Rovelli believes that we live in a fundamentally atemporal universe. We believe that in an atemporal universe retarded and advanced waves or some other form of pilot wave, would not be surprising, and might be expected. Even if pilot waves prove insufficient to describe reality, Rovelli strongly suggests that when we understand quantum gravity we will find that time, and perhaps space, are emergent, not fundamental. We find this line of thought to be the most promising path to a more complete model of our physical universe.

Quantum Entanglement

There are many possible models vastly more complex than Cramer's TI that represent what are essentially universes without fundamental space and time. Several are perhaps more likely to reflect reality than TI. Many incorporate quantum entanglement as a fundamental property of the theories.[286]

---

[283] John G. Cramer, "The Transactional Interpretation of Quantum Mechanics," (2015). http://arxiv.org/pdf/1503.00039.pdf
[284] Brian Dodson, "So You Think YOU'RE Confused About Quantum Mechanics?" *GizMag* (March 2013). http://www.gizmag.com/confusion-basic-nature-quantum-mechanics/26216/; Schlosshauer, Kofler, and Zeilinger, "A Snapshot of Foundational Attitudes Toward Quantum Mechanics."
[285] Carlo Rovelli, "Forget time," *Foundations of Physics* 41 (2011): 1475-1490. doi:10.1007/s10701-011-9561-4 [preprint http://arxiv.org/pdf/0903.3832.pdf]
[286] Lee Smolin, "Space: The Final Illusion," *Scientific American* (April 4, 2019). Retrieved from https://blogs.scientificamerican.com/observations/space-the-final-illusion/

If we are going to understand time and consciousness we need to find an explanation for the observed phenomena of quantum entanglement (QE). It is very early in the search for an understanding of QE. If QE is real, as recent experiments appear to verify, then the quest for the cause of spooky action at a distance is one of the most important scientific inquiries ahead of us,[287] as much so as finding quantum gravity. Until we acquire some understanding of the mechanism behind QE we only have speculative ideas about the nature of consciousness and the limits of physics.

The rational mind allows two intuitive answers for the phenomena of QE, the distance between two entangled particles is zero or the length of time for communications is zero (or both). It may be that there is some other totally unknown, possibly unknowable, "spooky" property of the universe that explains QE. Yet finding a model with no fundamental separation in which space and time are emergent, appears to be the best way to remain somewhat consistent with the known laws of physics.[288]

One of the interesting areas of inquiry is the idea that space-time may be a holographic projection of a 2 dimensional plane on which there is no separation.[289] The achronal boundary and adjacent layers associated with the event horizon of a black hole are possible (though to us intuitively unlikely) sources for

---

[287] We often hear that the usefulness of QE is to build quantum computers, that trivial view is rather like saying that we needed to understand fire so that we could build cigarette lighters.

[288] Smolin, Lee. "Space is Dead: A Challenge to the Standard Model of Quantum Mechanics," *EDGE, The Big Think*, August 25, 2019. https://bigthink.com/videos/lee-smolin-space. We don't believe that many of Smolin's ideas are correct, however we do think that there is a realistic mechanism where both time and space emerge from more fundamental causal events. Such a model appears to offer the only path to a rational explanation of quantum entanglement.

[289] Scientific American Video. "Is Our Universe a Hologram?" - https://youtu.be/gS3KWoO9yYA

such a projection.[290] It seems likely that to solve the mysteries of consciousness we will first need to understand QE's observed simultaneous two-way communication over almost infinite distances.

If there is no fundamental time and space, we may exist in a universe that has relative position and separation, with space and time being derived and not fundamental. Perhaps the universe is defined by something like the rather wild amplituhedron proposed by physicist Arkani-Hamed,[291] a physical structure that does not need space or time to describe our physical reality. Like Barbour, Arkani-Hamed posits an underlying rigid causal structure that allows for the experience of temporal evolution through construction of a relativistic space-time scaffold on a shape dynamic base. Or it may be that loop quantum gravity / spin-foam is the better theory, we simply don't know.[292]

We discussed the possibility of an atemporal universe along with the block universe because the structure of an atemporal universe resembles a block model. The difference is that slices of an atemporal block universe represent relative positions and not planes of simultaneity. No one really has any idea at all what the fundamental nature of our universe is. We may live in an atemporal universe, or the opposite, a universe with fundamental temporal causal structure. Both would support

[290] Gustavo E. Romero and Gabriela S. Vila, "Black Hole Physics" In *Introduction to Black Hole Astrophysics*, (Heidelberg: Springer Berlin, 2014), 73-97. http://arxiv.org/pdf/1409.3318.pdf We do not agree with Romero when he argues that the existence of black holes disproves presentism. Romero frames his arguments around simultaneity, which has no physical meaning in an atemporal model.

[291] N. Arkani-Hamed and J. Trnka, "The Amplituhedron," *Journal of High Energy Physics* (2014): 1-33. doi:10.1007/JHEP10(2014)030
[292] Rovelli, Carlo, and Francesca Vidotto. *Covariant Loop Quantum Gravity: An Elementary Introduction to Quantum Gravity and Spinfoam Theory.* Cambridge: Cambridge University Press, 2014. doi:10.1017/CBO9781107706910.

our conclusions[293] that after physical death we will experience a non-physical existence, or *nothing*.

---

[293] Some would argue the opposite is true, that an atemporal universe is closer to the eternalism we discuss in the next section. However atemporal eternalism, eternalism without time, would be no more than a neutral stage for sequential causal events that do not exist, exist, do not exist. That mechanism appears to be consistent with existence presentism.

Philosophical View of Time

Philosophers approach the idea of existence from a semantic viewpoint.[294] Dean Zimmerman[295] does an excellent job of sorting through the incredible complexities of tensed language, explaining the intricacies of A-theory and B-theory, and offering reasons why we might want to take tense seriously. We will look at why the role of tense in understanding existence is, to say the least, controversial and does not alter our conclusions.[296]

Eternalism

Eternalism is the philosophical equivalent of the block universe for the physicist who champions Einstein's relativity. It is the only philosophic position that is recognized as compatible with special relativity, general relativity, and some interpretations of quantum mechanics, and that is observer-independent.[297] Eternalism allows for the relativity of simultaneity which is at the core of Einstein's theories.

Presentism

Presentism is somewhat like the collapse of the wave equation, where a particular quantum value is determined only when observed.[298] The presentist believes that only the present is real, the past no longer exists and the future has not come into

---

[294] See in general Dean W. Zimmerman, *Prologue: Metaphysics After the Twentieth Century*, and in particular the chapter by D. Lewis, "Tensed Quantifiers," *Oxford Studies in Metaphysics* (Oxford: Oxford University Press, 2004).

[295] Dean W. Zimmerman, "The A-Theory of Time, The B-Theory of Time, and 'Taking Tense Seriously'," *Dialectica* 59 (2005): 401-457. doi:10.1111/j.1746-8361.2005.01041.x

[296] B. Lee, "Eternalism, Counting Across Times and the Argument from Semantics," *Inquiry* Forthcoming (2015). doi:10.1080/0020174X.2014.980754

[297] Fabien Besnard, "Is There a Philosophy of Time Compatible with Relativity and Quantum Mechanics?" In *Frontiers of Fundamental Physics: The Eleventh International Symposium* 1446 (2012): 437-447). doi:10.1063/1.4728010

[298] B. Monton, "Presentism and Quantum Gravity," *Philosophy and Foundations of Physics* (2006): 263-280.

being. Presentism and Newtonian time share a basic structure of fundamental time flowing from past to future.

Presentism is not necessarily compatible with the current understanding of relativity,[299] however we believe existence presentism would be consistent with an atemporal, perhaps an aspatial, interpretation of the universe. Presentism lost favor when Einstein declared that no events can be said to be absolutely simultaneous.[300] Yet presentism continues to have support among a small group of scientists who believe that relativity is incomplete or misinterpreted,[301] do not believe that relativity requires a block universe,[302] and/or believe that our understanding of temporality is misguided.[303] We will discuss existence presentism a bit later.

Possibilism

Possibilism is the philosophical equivalent of the evolving block universe[304] which accommodates the uncertainty principal of quantum physics by allowing an open future.[305] It is also consistent with special relativity and general relativity, but only if the past of an observer is taken as their causal past and closed timelike curves are forbidden so that the past cannot be

---

[299] Wuthrich, "The Fate of Presentism in Modern Physics".

[300] Ibid.

[301] E. Anderson, "Problem of Time in Quantum Gravity." *Annalen der Physik* 524 (2012): 757-786.

[302] Dean Zimmerman, "Presentism and the Space-Time Manifold," In *The Oxford Handbook of Philosophy of Time* (Oxford: Oxford University Press, 2011), 163-244.

[303] C. Wuthrich and C. Callender, "What Becomes of a Causal Set," (2015). arXiv preprint - http://arxiv.org/pdf/1502.00018v1.pdf

[304] George Ellis, "The Evolving Block Universe and the Meshing Together of Times." *Annals of the New York Academy of Sciences* 1326 (2014): 26-41. doi:10.1111/nyas.12559; George Ellis, "Time Really Exists! The Evolving Block Universe," Enuresis Journal 7 (2014): 11-26. We disagree with Ellis and Smolin. http://www.euresisjournal.org/public/issue/pdf/EuresisJournal-issue7.pdf

[305] Vladislav E. Terekhovich, "Modal Approaches in Metaphysics and Quantum Mechanics," (2015). http://philsci-archive.pitt.edu/11319/1/ModalityInQM.pdf

altered.[306] The evolving block universe seems to accommodate the fixed past of relativity and the uncertain future of quantum theory, but in fact it inherits the problems of both eternalism and presentism.[307]

Who is Right?

While we would like to help the reader slog through the philosophical issues, we believe that understanding the physics is a better way to evaluate the discussion of existence. Callendar argues strongly that eternalism, presentism, and possibilism are equivalent, or at least not helpful, in understanding time. Essentially his argument is that the three metaphysical positions are empirically equivalent to one another, explanatorily equivalent to one another, and perhaps even metaphysically equivalent to one another.[308] In all three models we experience a present that is recognized but not explained by any of the theories.

Callender sees the need for philosophy to look at what must be explained, examine the science, and then try to account for any explanatory gap.[309] In other words, the real problem is not the existence of past, present, and future events, but rather is explaining our daily experience of the flow of time.[310] In our earlier chapter on time we explained why we favor an atemporal presentism, specifically a form of existence presentism. If our conclusions are right Callender's arguments would need to be revisited in light of the physical reality of some form of existence presentism.

---

[306] Ibid.

[307] John Earman, "Pruning Some Branches from 'Branching Spacetimes'," In ed. Dennis Dieks, *The Ontology of Spacetime II* (New York: Elsevier, 2008), 187-205.

[308] Craig Callender. "Time's Ontic Voltage," In ed. Adrian Bardon, *The Future of the Philosophy of Time*, (New York: Routeledge, 2012), 73-98.

[309] Ibid.

[310] Smolin, *Time Reborn: From the Crisis in Physics to the Future of the Universe.* We don't agree with Smolin's ideas about the role of time in cosmology.

If we live in a block universe then there is a "you" that exists on your worldline for every event in your physical life, there is no singular physical you. If we live in an infinite number of parallel universes, then there is no singular physical you who survives your physical / natural death. In both cases there would be billions of isolated "you's" either lying along your worldline or stuck somewhere in totally isolated universes. If we live in an atemporal universe the physical /natural you will cease to exist on your physical / natural death. None of these possibilities offer us a permanent individual physical / natural consciousness. It is equally true that they have nothing to say about the possibility of a non-physical existence after physical death.

Existential Meaning and Science

There is a third possible alternative to the block theory / eternalism and the atemporal theory / presentism, *existentialism*.[311] Existentialism is critically viewed as a cultural movement rather than a philosophical position. That is why we defined our use of the term as meaning "in and of itself", to avoid the popular view as an historic artifact. The broad idea is that physical life has meaning and value in and of itself, without a life after death. Modern philosophies grounded in existentialist principles are championed by neuroexistentialists, realists, and humanists. Some form of existentialism is necessarily a fundamental belief of any human being who lives their life without expectation of an afterlife.

We cannot rule out the possibility we live in an existential world, if for no other reason than the fact that it is arguably (setting aside formal logic) impossible to prove a negative. In other words, we might be able to prove that physical consciousness after death exists in the universe by observing it, but we can never prove that permanent physical consciousness, natural consciousness, or some other form of existential meaning, does not exist after death because we have not observed it. Indeed, the very fact that human beings exist in our universe argues for existential meaning and purpose.[312] Perhaps there is some singular physical, or non-physical consciousness constrained by natural laws (a permanent natural consciousness), that incorporates all of the events along our worldline, and that preserves our physical past, present, and future. If we have a physical or natural existence that has

---

[311] Steven Crowell, "Existentialism", *The Stanford Encyclopedia of Philosophy* (Winter 2017 Edition), Edward N. Zalta (ed.), https://plato.stanford.edu/archives/win2017/entries/existentialism/ .

[312] Gary T. Reker, "Theoretical Perspective, Dimensions, and Measurement of Existential Meaning," In *Exploring Existential Meaning: Optimizing Human Development across the Life Span* (Thousand Oaks, CA: Sage Publications, 2000), 39-55; Paul Wong, ed. *The Human Quest for Meaning: Theories, Research, and Applications* (London: Routledge, 2013).

existential meaning then the billions of people who intuitively believe that every day, every moment, of their lives has purpose and value are absolutely right.

Yet if we are to believe that there may be some kind of singular physical or natural consciousness that survives physical death, then it would seem we would need to accept that there is some unique physical or natural consciousness that is "me", incorporates all of the conscious events of my life, and is somehow not dependent on the physical existence of my biologic body and/or natural existence of my mind. Current interpretations of theories do not rule out the possibility of a perpetual individual physical consciousness, or a perpetual natural consciousness which is a fundamental part of the universe and constrained by natural laws. Yet there is no known method that is both rational and realistic (i.e. - a theory that appears capable of modeling physical reality) to construct a physical and/or natural consciousness (as opposed to a non-physical) model that permanently preserves the singular human consciousness of an individual after the physical / natural death of that person.

Modern theories suggest the possibility that multiple instances of a physical "me" exist in space-time or in parallel universes, but they do not tell us how to unite all of those instances into a single physical "me" whose consciousness spans space-time. It is equally true that there is no rational and realistic theory that would unite multiple instances of an immaterial consciousness constrained by natural laws, each instance of which supervenes on a physical "me". It is very difficult to believe that a soul exists which is constrained by natural laws yet is somehow permanent. Furthermore, no theory exists, and none seems possible, that preserves singular physical consciousness, or immaterial consciousness constrained by the laws of nature, beyond the current epoch in which the universe supports sentience. Indeed, canonical interpretations of quantum superposition seem to deny the possibility of a single physical or natural reality.[313]

---

[313] Dorato, "Events and the Ontology of Quantum Mechanics".

It also seems intuitively unlikely that a single universal consciousness constrained by natural laws (not a non-physical, independent, individual consciousness not subject to the laws of physics or nature) would in any meaningful way preserve the individual consciousness of billions of human beings. If a natural universal consciousness evolved according to laws of nature there would be no reason to believe that evolutionary mechanisms would preserve immaterial individual consciousness that does not supervene on a physical being.

There would be no evolutionary benefit to conferring permanence on individual or universal immaterial consciousness, the evolutionary purpose of which was to supervene on the physical and improve the odds of survival of the species, not the individual. Just as the physical being exists from birth to death, it would seem that we have no reason to believe that an immaterial consciousness that supervenes on the physical would not also exist from physical birth to, at most, a finite time shortly after physical death. As we have said, even if it existed beyond physical death, it is virtually impossible to believe that such an immaterial consciousness constrained by the laws of nature would continue to exist during the inevitable epoch(s) that will not support sentience.

The possibility of a permanent physical or natural consciousness appears to require the existence of a physical and/or natural consciousness that is not bound to events on a worldline. Yet it seems intuitively true that if consciousness of past events can be lost when memories fade in old age or are damaged when we suffer brain injuries or strokes, then physical or natural consciousness has not have incorporated those past events into a permanent singular "me". In fact, every night between dreams we lose touch with our past memories as we sleep. Einstein only briefly addressed physical (not necessarily non-physical) existence when he said "An individual who should survive his physical death is also beyond my comprehension."[314]

---

[314] Albert Einstein. *The World as I See It*. (San Diego: Book Tree, 2007), 5.

While we can visualize and accept a "non-physical independent consciousness" that survives physical death,[315] we are unable to have any confidence in the existence of a singular physical or natural consciousness that permanently survives the physical death of a human being. We may be wrong. Almost every philosopher and scientist, in fact almost all of the billions of human beings who live on this earth, believe that physical life has existential meaning and purpose. We can say that after many, many years of thought we are convinced that any attempt to construct a model of permanent physical or natural consciousness does more damage to the centuries of accumulated scientific knowledge, than does the acceptance of the possibility that a permanent non-physical independent consciousness may exist. Yet our intuition may be telling us that physical life does in fact have existential meaning which has not yet been explained, or at least not satisfactorily explained, by science.

In coming out of the dark ages human beings have made enormous intellectual leaps in philosophy and science, so much so that many now believe we understand how life works. We need to recognize the fact that when future generations look back at twenty-first century science it will seem as primitive to them as alchemy does to us, and they will be rightly amazed at our lack of understanding of our existence. There are glimpses of a possible future which might provide a theoretical foundation for existential consciousness and might give meaning to our lives in ways that we cannot yet imagine. Yet at this point these speculative ideas about the existence of a permanent physical and/or natural consciousness are little more than scientific and philosophical fiction, there is no objective or intuitive reason to believe that any of them will be found to give meaning to human existence.

Transhumanism

---

[315] Larry Dossey, "Should Clinicians Honor Immortality? Reflections on the Continuity of Consciousness," *Spirituality in Clinical Practice* 1 (2014): 184. doi:10.1037/scp0000026 Dossey appears to favor a form of universal physical consciousness/pantheism that we have problems with.

A brief comment on those (transhumanists) who believe they may be able to physically perpetuate themselves through cryogenics, cloning, etc.[316] If theories that predict endless cycles of expansion and contraction of our universe are correct, nothing physical (natural) can survive beyond the next collapse of the universe a few billion years from today. While that may seem absurdly far away, your great, great, great (to the 100th. power), grand-clone would find it frightfully real when the time came for the collapse, a distant time from now which like all imaginable time is but a second in eternity.

On the other hand, if we live in a constantly expanding universe, our universe will eventually return to a state of uniformly high entropy. It is generally accepted that in the very distant future, as entropy increases, the cosmos will become a hostile environment in which physical life cannot be sustained. In both the case where the universe collapses and the case where it reaches maximal entropy, transhumanism[317] appears to be an irrational, totally empty, promise. There is no cosmologic model that we know of that offers any hope for a perpetual, physical, human existence.

What about continued existence of an immaterial human consciousness which is a fundamental part of the universe? It is very difficult to imagine an immaterial self-aware mind that exists within the observable universe without a physical body. We have no objective scientific observations of what is essentially a "ghost" which we can have any confidence in. There is some evidence of psychic telepathy and pre-cognition,[318] but non-

---

[316] Calvin Mercer & Tracy J. Trothen, eds. *Religion and Transhumanism: The Unknown Future of Human Enhancement* (Santa Barbara: Praeger, 2015); William R. Stoeger and G. F. R. Ellis, "A Response to Tipler's Omega-Point Theory," *Science and Christian Belief* 7 (1995): 163-72. From http://www.joly.org.uk/gordo/ellis3.html

[317] Using technology to enhance human physical, intellectual, and psychological capacities, eventually leading to reincarnation into robotic bodies.

[318] Daryl J. Bem, "Feeling the Future: Experimental Evidence for Anomalous Retroactive Influences on Cognition and Affect." *Journal of*

physical connections between two conscious human beings who physically exist in the universe is intuitively vastly different from communication with immaterial consciousness that has no physical being to embody.[319]

There is no question that many people think they experience what is known as after-death communication,[320] yet after many years of trying to prove the existence of psychic communications with the dead there is no study that validates a connection between a living person and an immaterial independent consciousness that once supervened on a person who is now physically dead. There certainly is no credible evidence that if such an immaterial consciousness existed as a fundamental part of the universe, it would preserve meaningful individual human consciousness or that it would survive those periods in cosmological history which are hostile to the existence of any sentient beings. We simply have no intuitive reason to believe in the existence of a permanent immaterial human consciousness which is a fundamental part of the universe and constrained by the laws of nature. This does not in any way diminish the possibility of a non-physical independent consciousness, a soul, not constrained by physical and/or natural laws.

Even if in some unknown manner multiple clones could survive in an ever-expanding universe, the idea that they are

---

Personality and Social Psychology 100, no. 3 (2011): 407-425. doi:10.1037/a0021524; Steve Taylor, "Do Psychic Phenomena Exist?" *Psychology Today*, (Apr 16, 2014). www.psychologytoday.com/blog/out-the-darkness/201404/do-psychic-phenomena-exist-0

[319] Kurtz, Paul. "The New Paranatural Paradigm: Claims of Communicating with the Dead." *Skeptical Inquirer* 24, no. 6 (2000): 28. http://www.csicop.org/si/show/new_paranatural_paradigm_claims_of_communicating_with_the_dead/

[320] Jenny Streit-Horn, *A Systematic Review of Research on After-Death Communication (ADC),*. (Denton, Texas: UNT Digital Library, 2011) . http://digital.library.unt.edu/ark:/67531/metadc84284/

perpetual extensions of their donor seems less than credible.[321] Such a perpetual presence seems to be more like an endless path of meaningless individual moments experienced by many physical me's, than a continuous meaningful existence experienced by one "me". Furthermore, if there is no non-physical life after death, it would make no difference if an individual (cloned or otherwise) continued to exist, or "died" in one hundred years or in one billion years, because "death" would annihilate the individual's past, present, and future.

Revisiting Non-Physical Consciousness - Independent

What objective evidence do we have that the consciousness of the mind is not dependent on the physical brain? There is evidence that points to non-locality and the quantum mind as sources of consciousness. However, the proof is tentative and could fall like a house of cards. As far as we can tell, there is no rational answer to the fundamental nature of consciousness, or for that matter, of the universe.

The best current overview of consciousness is Litchfield's article in the April 2015 Atlantic magazine, where he concludes that "the question of how consciousness emerges is in fact likely to be one of the defining problems of the 21st century."[322] Even his balanced review assumes without objective foundation that NDE's are likely to be found to have physical origins. If near death experiences have a physical origin, it would not prove or disprove the existence of non-physical consciousness after physical death. If the source of NDE's and/or other non-physical consciousness is beyond human observation, science cannot prove them to be true or false, or say anything objective at all about their reality. For now we continue to rely, at least in part, on intuition.

Intuition

---

[321] John Gray, *The Immortalization Commission: Science and the Strange Quest to Cheat Death* (New York: Macmillan, 2011).
[322] Lichfield, "The Science of Near-Death Experiences."

We talked about science[323] and philosophy,[324] and suggested that neither has given us a satisfactory answer to our questions about consciousness and existence. We suggested that common sense, innate beliefs, observations, subjective deductions, what we might call intuitions, may offer the best available answers. We noted that what is intuitively true may or may not be factually true, and that future scientific and philosophical inquiry might cast doubt on what we intuitively believe to be true. Yet we suggested that we are justified in basing conclusions on those best evidence intuitive feelings. What we intuitively believe to be true may in fact be true.

What value is intuition in our inquiries? At first thought intuition seems like a guess, or as is often said in academia, a prejudice without empirical support. It is true that intuition can be based on unsupported feelings, but it can be more than that.[325] Einstein once said about science, "I believe in intuitions and inspirations. I sometimes feel that I am right. I do not know that I am." "... I am enough of the artist to draw freely upon my imagination. Imagination is more important than knowledge. Knowledge is limited. Imagination encircles the world."[326]

The philosopher Saul Kripke said "Of course, some philosophers think that something's having intuitive content is very inconclusive evidence in favor of it. I think it is very heavy evidence in favor of anything, myself. I really don't know, in a way, what more conclusive evidence one can have about anything,

---

[323] Woit, *Not Even Wrong: The Failure of String Theory and the Continuing Challenge to Unify the Laws of Physics.*

[324] Peter Unger, *Empty Ideas: A Critique of Analytic Philosophy* (Oxford: Oxford University Press, 2014).

[325] David Chalmers, "Intuitions in Philosophy: A Minimal Defense," *Philosophical Studies* 171 (2014): 535-544; Elijah Chudnoff, "The Nature of Intuitive Justification." *Philosophical Studies* 153 (2011): 313-333; Elijah Chudnoff, *Intuition* (Oxford: Oxford University Press, 2013).

[326] George S. Viereck, "What Life Means to Einstein: An Interview by George Sylvester Viereck," *Saturday Evening Post*, (October 26, 1929). http://www.saturdayeveningpost.com/wp-content/uploads/satevepost/what_life_means_to_einstein.pdf

ultimately speaking."[327] Perhaps Kripke is saying that since we cannot know anything with absolute certainty what can be better than our best intuition of what is true based on our scientific and philosophic knowledge?

Part of the problem is in failing to understand that intuition can be understood across a range from unsupported feelings to rationally interpreted observations.[328] The key is a discriminative use of intuition.[329] For example, the weight as empirical evidence that we might give to reports by those who intuitively believe they have experienced an abduction by aliens is of a different nature to the intuitive belief that we cannot go back to yesterday and live it over again.

If we ask ourselves is it intuitively likely that we can go back and redo the conscious experiences of yesterday, the answer is no. We can imagine being the same human being, going into the same room, and sitting in the same chair we did yesterday, but we intuitively "know" that we have not traveled back to yesterday. If we painted a red line on the floor last night, we know that if not erased since that event, it will be there when we enter the room today. We intuitively know that we cannot change our mind, go back, and for the first time paint a blue line instead of a red line.

The theoretical possibility of closed time-like curves in a block universe prevents us from saying that time travel to the past is scientifically impossible. We can offer technical arguments that it is in fact impossible but we lack objective proof of our assertions.[330] The theoretical possibility of time travel is not convincing evidence for us against the majority's intuition that time travel is not possible, that we cannot return to yesterday and do it over again. Of course, our intuition about time may turn out to be wrong, or it may be right. It is not the intuition that

---

[327] Saul Kripke, *Naming and Necessity* (Cambridge, MA: Harvard University Press, 1980): 40.
[328] Roger, Penrose, "Penrose Talks about When We Need to Sidestep Reason," YouTube video., (2008). https://youtu.be/xiYDc1LA0I4
[329] John Bengson, "How Philosophers Use Intuition and 'Intuition'," *Philosophical Studies* 171 (2014). doi:10.1007/s11098-014-0287-y
[330] See Michael Kaku, http://mkaku.org/home/articles/the-physics-of-time-travel/

determines the truth or falsity of time travel, it is reality that does that.[331]

What is the empirical weight of our intuitive evidence supporting presentism? Given the collective observations of human beings over the millennia of the passage of yesterday to today to tomorrow, and the lack of any evidentiary consensus that being and becoming do not occur, the empirical weight of our intuition seems rather high. That does not mean that we are correct, but absent compelling scientific or philosophical evidence to the contrary, we can be confident in our belief that our physical existence sequentially moves forward from physical birth to physical death.

Does our belief support an intuitive conclusion that physical death is the end of consciousness? An intuitive belief that physical consciousness ends with physical death seems to be as reasonable as our intuitive belief about the passage of time. However intuitive evidence for the end of *physical consciousness* at physical death is not the same as the intuitive evidence for the end of *consciousness* at physical death.

We can observe the effects of physical death on physical consciousness, there is no intuitive feeling that a thousand-year-old skeleton is physically conscious. It seems that our intuitive belief that physical consciousness ends at physical death constitutes strong empirical evidence. Yet we have no observations that support or deny non-physical consciousness after physical death. Indeed anecdotal, often claimed to be objective, evidence for and against non-physical consciousness seems weak.

The difference in the empirical weight we might give to the intuitive belief that physical consciousness passes from yesterday to today to tomorrow, and the weight we give to the intuitive belief that we have a non-physical consciousness, is found in the

---

[331] A. Higgins, *The Nature of Intuitions and Their Role in Material Object Metaphysics,* Doctoral dissertation. (2015) From http://hdl.handle.net/2142/72936; Jennifer Nado, "Why intuition?" *Philosophy and Phenomenological Research* 89 (2014): 15-41. doi: 10.1111/phpr.644

fact that all human beings observe what they agree to be the passage of time while only some observe what they believe to be non-physical consciousness. The lack of universal intuitive support for non-physical consciousness does not offer empirical evidence for or against the existence of non-physical consciousness. If non-physical consciousness does exist it may well be entirely beyond human ability to observe during our physical lifetimes.

Two Big Questions

There is nothing new about what we have been saying, we have not even introduced a novel approach.[332] What we have done is identify lines of thought that seem to us to be persuasive and taken them to their logical conclusions. One thing that has kept us interested over the years is the search for answers to two fundamental questions posited by this book. By looking at the questions we will focus on, and offer a summary of, the consequences we have talked about. Many have thought the same thoughts, not many have taken the concepts to their logical extremes. After you finish reading our book you will be better prepared to reach your own personal conclusions.

Consciousness Requires Physical Existence

The first big question is whether the physical and/or natural existence of a human being is necessary for that person to experience physical and/or natural consciousness?[333] We discussed how physical consciousness (brain), and if it exists immaterial natural consciousness (mind), are considered by most philosophers and scientists[334] to be fundamental properties of the universe constrained by physical / natural laws. We noted that both are very different from an independent consciousness beyond physical and natural properties which is not dependent on the existence of the universe.[335]

If Einstein's general relativity is correct, then we may live in a block universe and it might not matter if consciousness

---

[332] Camus and Nietzsche reach similar conclusions, but then out of apparent despair they collapsed into existential humanism, something we think is unsupported and unnecessary.

[333] Our classifications (1) Physical Consciousness – Dependent and (2) Physical / Natural Consciousness – Independent.

[334] Scientists who accept the possibility that the brain / mind are independent and that the immaterial mind is unknown but not unknowable, so that in the future the immaterial mind can be a proper subject of subjective scientific inquiry.

[335] Our classification (3) Non-Physical Consciousness – Independent.

depends on existence because existence never ends.[336] The underlying question is whether existence is a sequential process where Event A → Event B → Event C → Event D → Event E is true in that causal order so that only one Event can be said to exist (presentism), or whether all Events exist (eternalism-block universe).

The block universe, which is usually said to be a consequence of relativity, requires that events A | B | C | D | E simply exist. The expanding block universe says that perhaps A | B | C exist, however if we are experiencing Event C, then A | B | C → Event D → Event E is true. In other words, the past is fixed and permanent, but the future is uncertain. A similar view suggests that we live in an evolving block universe, where A | B | C | D | E exist but it is also true that there is becoming, there is sequential being from Event A |→ Event B |→ Event C |→ Event D |→ Event E. The past, present, and future A | B | C | D | E are fixed and permanent, but it is also true that objects sequentially pass from A→ Event B → Event C → Event D → Event E.

While the expanding block universe seems possible, it is very difficult to comprehend an evolving block universe where all past, present, and future events exist and where we "travel" from one event to the next event. No matter which seems more probable, both the expanding and the evolving block universes identify a preferred "now". Any model having one event which in any sense is "now" violates relativity, so both models are rejected by most relativists. Furthermore, our present understanding of quantum probabilities appears incompatible with any block universe.

A different possibility is that each event is exclusive in the sense of excluding the existence of past and future events as part of the set of all events (a form of existence presentism). Each event occurs in a sequential (not temporal), causal order, Event A → Event B → Event C → Event D → Event E. Here is where we part

---

[336] Michael Silberstein, W. M. Stuckey, and Timothy McDevitt, "Being, Becoming and the Undivided Universe: A Dialogue Between Relational Blockworld and the Implicate Order Concerning the Unification of Relativity and Quantum Theory," *Foundations of Physics* 43 (2013): 502-532. doi:10.1007/s10701-012-9653-9

from the classical understanding by concluding that Event C does NOT EXIST, Event C does EXIST, Event C does NOT EXIST as part of the set of all events. There is no good way to visualize this idea, because if Event C EXISTS then Event A, B, D, and E are *nothing*.

We adopt the inadequate convention ~~Event A~~ → ~~Event B~~ → Event C → ~~Event D~~ → ~~Event E~~, and say that past events (and in some sense future events) are consumed by *nothing*.[337] Again there is no description, mathematical or otherwise, that is adequate to describe the *nothing* in the sequential causal order preceding and proceeding Event C. Existence presentism expands the concept of an event by positing a more complex "present" with "momentary" duration,[338] similar to the idea of composite worldtubes, so that Event C would occupy a tiny area but not just a point in space-time.[339]

In some existence presentism models, Event C is made up of a set of observable physical objects x, x^1, x^2, x^3, x^4, ... that exist Event C = $[x, x^1, x^2, x^3, x^4, ...]$.[340] Event B may "have contained" (tensed language has no place in our examples other than for familiar simplicity) some of those objects (Event B = $[x, x^1]$), but Event B itself never equals, or even exists in the same universe as, Event C. This idea of the persistence of objects in emergent space that evolves sequentially, not temporally, is a powerful interpretation of relativity and quantum theory that, at least on the surface, does not violate core principals of either one. What it does do is offer a new perspective on physical existence that

---

[337] There are other more difficult ways to understand the absence of Events A, B, D, E from the set of all events, for our purposes any logically consistent reason for only one Event C being real supports our conclusions.

[338] Temporal terms like momentary are used for convenience, however the expanded event of existence presentism is essentially atemporal and consists of a tiny bounded volume of spacetime defined by relative positions, it is not a point of space or a period of time.

[339] Vesselin. "Time and Reality of Worldtubes."

[340] Some texts describe Event C as a set of multiple "sub" events $[c_1, c_2, c_3, c_4, ...]$.

solves paradoxes and supports the conclusion that Event C does NOT EXIST, Event C does EXIST, Event C does NOT EXIST.

We have discussed the fact that most physicists believe general relativity requires a block universe, and that quantum theory requires, at a minimum, that a fully realized past universe expand or evolve. If we set existence presentism to the side for the moment, and take what would seem to be the best case for a permanent physical consciousness, a block universe that includes all past events, then do we have a model where our consciousness is permanently fixed in space-time? We simply do not because if we live in a block universe, literally billions of discrete, very real, versions of each of us occupy space-time or multiple universes, no single one of which is "you".

Would the existence of immaterial natural consciousness help us? We have said that the natural consciousness philosophers and some scientists are talking about is constrained by known, and unknown but knowable,[341] fundamental laws of nature. Natural consciousness associated with a brain / mind would embody a physical being while they physically exist, while universal consciousness would encompass all that is without regard to individual consciousness. There is no evolutionary benefit or other intuitive reason why natural or universal consciousness would be expected to preserve individual consciousness after physical death. Furthermore, it is intuitively true that a physical consciousness, and/or an immaterial consciousness constrained by the laws of nature, could not survive the inevitable cosmologic epochs during which no sentience can be expected to exist. There simply is no rational reason to believe that an immaterial natural or universal consciousness would provide us with a permanent individual consciousness.

What if Newton was right and the flow of time is in fact a fundamental property of the universe,[342] would that preserve

---

[341] Knowable in the sense of being fundamental properties of the universe, which may or may not be known in the future by human beings.

[342] Smolin, *Time Reborn.*

human consciousness? If this is how reality works we live in a now, today, which will no longer exist tomorrow.[343] Our statement that after a comet destroyed the Earth there would be no conscious beings who even knew it struck their planet, would be more likely, not less likely, to be true. If the flow of time is a fundamental property of the universe then the possibility of *nothing* seems even more reasonable.

We discussed another, existential, possibility, that consciousness does not require physical / natural existence and is permanent. We found it to be the weakest of all in terms of both rational objective and intuitive support. Acceptance of a permanent existential consciousness is deeply rooted in evolutionary design, yet there is no credible evidence whatsoever that it is a property of reality.[344] It is logically more reasonable to accept the possibility of a non-physical existence after physical death that is beyond human observation than it is to accept the possibility of a meaningful physical / natural existential existence constrained by physical and natural laws, for which no objective scientific evidence has been found in the observable world. The idea that human consciousness has permanent meaning apart from the existence of human beings seems to be an empty claim without scientific, philosophic, or other rational foundation.

---

[343] Newton's flow of time is actually another way to describe presentism.

[344] Barash says "It is well known that existentialists are very much occupied with the meaninglessness of life, and with the consequent need for people to assert their own meaning, to define themselves against an absurd universe that dictates that ultimately, everything will come to naught, because they will die. Less well known is the assertion by evolutionary biologists and existentialists alike that life is truly absurd." David P. Barash, "Evolutionary Existentialism, Sociobiology, and the Meaning of Life" *BioScience* 50, no.11 (2000): 1012-1017. Unwilling to recognize *nothing* and to accept the possibility of life after physical death, he joins the existentialists in vainly trying to create something.

We intuitively favor a form of existence presentism,[345] where complex, atemporal,[346] events[347] are all that exist. There is no reason to believe that the myths of humanism are true.[348] Our conclusion is the opposite of the humanist, neuroexistentialist, realist movement. It seems to go against scientific logic, but it actually rejects a simplistic understanding of philosophy and science. You may not yet agree with us, but if you objectively analyze our arguments you should eventually see why we strongly believe we are right.

Our answer to the first question is that physical / natural consciousness (not non-physical independent consciousness) requires physical and/or natural existence. Our conclusion is that physical / natural consciousness is at best temporary.[349] At some point in each of our causal futures it is true that: I am no longer a conscious, individual, human being; I do not exist; I have no past, present, or future that is my past, present, or future (if this is disturbing to you please read or reread The Possibility of *Nothing* and the Appendix).

Consciousness Requires Non-Physical Existence

---

[345] Tallant, "Defining Existence Presentism."

[346] Rovelli, "Forget Time."

[347] Vesselin. "Time and Reality of Worldtubes."

[348] Lonnie W. Aarssen, "Darwinism and Meaning," *Biological Theory* 5, no. 4 (2010): 296-311. While Aarssen does not consider the consequences of *nothing*, he agrees that humanism is a myth. We disagree with his assumption that there is no life after death, evolution does not require any conclusion about an afterlife. Because independent non-physical consciousness is beyond human observation no one can say anything objective about existence after physical death, so his assumptions about religion are unsupported. Nonetheless his analysis of the consequences of Darwinism and humanism is insightful and should be read with a discerning eye.

[349] Though we don't think so, perhaps the solipsists are right and human consciousness is just an illusion, as Einstein said "the separation between past, present, and future is only an illusion, although a convincing one." Polkinghorne, *Theology in the Context of Science*, 58.

The second big question, is it rational to believe in non-physical consciousness that exists after the death of our physical body? The trivial answer is that even science recognizes the unknown when it makes pronouncements about dark matter and energy. But what we really want to know is whether we are being rational when we believe in the existence of the non-physical which is beyond human observation.

If by rational we require proof, then we know that we cannot prove anything exists or does not exist beyond the limit of human observation. Yet we have already noted that the reason we cannot prove anything non-physical exists is not because nothing in fact does exist beyond the limit of human observation, but rather because we cannot know if anything exists or does not exist. Since that which we observe may be subject to forces beyond our observable world, we cannot make any objective statements about whether we will or will not have a non-physical existence beyond physical death. For that reason alone, we cannot conclude that it is irrational to accept the possibility that something *may* exist beyond human observation.

Recall that physical consciousness obeys physical laws and immaterial natural consciousness obeys natural laws, both are properties of the universe and dependent on it for their existence. Both physical and natural consciousness require existence in a universe conducive to sentient life. Independent non-physical consciousness is not dependent on or constrained by existence in a universe conducive to sentient life.

There is further support for our conclusion that there may be existence beyond human observation and that we may have a non-physical consciousness after physical death. Roger Penrose calculated that the creation of a universe in which we could exist required the selection of 1 universe out of 10 raised to the 10th power raised to the 123rd power ($10^{10^{123}}$) of all possible universes.[350] This is a deceptively large number, which in fact cannot be written. If you tried to write it out by writing the number 1 on a piece of paper, you would have to write a 0 on

[350] Penrose, *The Emperor's New Mind*, pp. 339-345. For a detailed explanation of how he calculated the odds see: http://www.ws5.com/Penrose/

every single atom in the universe just to approach the number of zeros that follow the 1, even then you would not be close to writing out the entire number.

This led Penrose, who is an agnostic and a patron of the British Humanist Society, to further conclude "There is a certain sense in which I would say the universe has a purpose. It's not there just somehow by chance. Some people take the view that the universe is simply there and it runs along... and we happen by accident to find ourselves in this thing. I don't think that's a very fruitful or helpful way of looking at the universe, I think that there is something much deeper about it, about its existence, which we have very little inkling of at the moment."[351] Most physicists find his calculations, if not 100% correct, compelling for the proposition that the existence of our universe cannot have occurred by chance. Note that the odds of selection of our universe out of all possible universes at the "big bang" is completely different from the odds of biological life spontaneously arising, you must have a universe conducive to life before you can even discuss the odds of life emerging in that universe.[352]

Rees and Smolin have tried to explain the almost impossible selection of the six fundamental constants and the initial condition of our universe as being the result of chance.[353] Their argument does not seem to address Penrose's initial

---

[351] Stephen Hawking and Roger Penrose appeared: In *A Brief History of Time*, motion picture, directed by Errol Morris (Original Release 1991, Triton Pictures, 2014, DVD in The Criterion Collection).

[352] Don't confuse the apples and oranges arguments that *life* arose in our universe as the result of random chance (Bayes formula - the average number of origin-of-life events for a given planet = [number of building blocks on planet] × 1/[average - mean] number of building blocks needed per "organism"] × [availability of building blocks during time t] × [probability of assembly in a given time] × time.) with the virtual impossibility that a *universe* conducive to life could be the result of random chance ($10^{10^{123}}$).

[353] Rees, *Just Six Numbers: The Deep Forces That Shape the Universe*; Smolin, *Time Reborn*.

selection calculation. Along with Penrose and others[354] we believe that science has shown us that the odds are almost infinitesimally small that our existence is the result of random selection, and that the logical conclusion is that our universe cannot be the product of chance. The rational, objective, conclusion is that our finely tuned universe and our own existence are the result of intelligent choice of which we have no scientific understanding.

Human beings have very little, we would say no, scientific inkling of how intelligent choice might exist outside the known laws of physics. Indeed, it appears that the origin of such intelligence may be beyond human observation, and perhaps comprehension. We simply cannot scientifically say anything about the nature of that which is beyond human observation. The apparent fact that our finely tuned universe is the result of intelligent choice lends additional intuitive support for our conclusion that independent non-physical consciousness may exist outside the constraints of physical and natural laws, and that we may in fact experience a conscious life after physical death.

---

[354] Alister E. McGrath, *A Fine-Tuned Universe: The Quest for God in Science and Theology: The 2009 Gifford Lectures,* No. 71. (Louisville: Westminster John Knox Press, 2009).

Finite Physical or Infinite Non-physical Consciousness

We have concluded, rightly or wrongly, that no current, or reasonably foreseeable, rational theory appears to provide us with a singular physical consciousness that continues to exist after physical death, so that a single physical "me" continues to exist after my death in my physical "past". We concluded that there is no reason to believe that physical and/or natural consciousness permanently exists after our physical death. If our physical and/or natural consciousness depends on our physical and/or natural existence, then at some point after our physical death we do not exist, *nothing*.

We have reached the point in our journey where we conclude that, like our pet rock, both our physical existence / consciousness and any natural existence / consciousness constrained by the laws of nature, is temporary. If our existence is constrained by the physical and natural laws of the universe, then our intuitive conclusion[355] is that on our physical death, *nothing*. We are ready to summarize what we have discussed in this book, and to consider in our other books our belief in the possibility of an independent non-physical consciousness not dependent on the physical / natural universe for its existence.

---

[355] Consistent with Occam's razor.

Final Comment

The intelligence that selected the initial conditions is attributed by most to God (see our other books for a lengthy discussion of the meaning of life and the existence of God – online and in Kindle, Google Books, and Apple formats: http://www.ws5.com).

The rational, objective, logical, conclusion for us is that God exists, or *nothing*.

If existence does not end at physical death, then life has meaning and purpose. There are three reasonable possibilities when we experience physical death:

1) our consciousness continues to exist in a positive state which many call heaven:

2) our consciousness continues to exist in a negative state which many call hell: or

3) *nothing.*

There may or may not be a non-physical existence after death, but there is every reason to live the most positive physical life possible, knowing that there is a rational possibility, no matter how slight, that there is a non-physical life after death.[356] There is no reason not to live the best possible life that we can, with the belief / faith[357] that there may be conscious life after physical death (if you don't understand our reasoning please reread The Possibility of Nothing). If there is non-physical existence after death then we have lived a meaningful life which will continue after physical death. If there is no non-physical existence after death then, *nothing.*

Having faith that we continue to exist after physical death is "infinitely" more rational than trying to do the impossible, make something out of *nothing.*

Appendix

---

[356] Nancey C. Murphy, *Theology in the Age of Scientific Reasoning,* (Ithaca: Cornell University Press, 1993).

[357] A stronger form of belief, see our other books for a detailed discussion of belief and faith.

Distress & Depression

DEPRESSION IS A MEDICAL CONDITION, IF YOU ARE DEPRESSED, FOR ANY REASON, YOU MUST SEEK PROFESSIONAL HELP NOW!

We have received comments from readers who tell us that our ideas caused them to be distressed or depressed. If you are one of those readers, you need to consider the following. As human beings become anxious they often lose their focus and objectivity, and misinterpret what they are reading. This is especially true if you are searching for meaning in your life, you do not believe that there is a life after death, and you are discouraged or depressed before you start reading. If you understand what we are saying, there is absolutely no reason to be distressed or depressed or even concerned by our ideas.

Why not? First, our conclusions may be right, we may have a permanent non-physical consciousness which gives meaning to life. Second, we may be wrong, life may have permanent existential meaning and value without a life after death. Third, if there is *nothing* after physical death you are absolutely free to live a life filled with both pain and joy, knowing that if you die today, or next year, or ten years from now, the pain will be as if it never was. No matter which of the three is right, depression, distress, and suicide destroy the possibility of finding the meaning and purpose which may in fact exist in each and every human being's life.

Beyond the fact that we cannot be sure we are right, nothing we have said changes the fact that all human beings can choose to do that which is good and live as positive a life as they can with the belief / faith that life may have meaning and purpose. It is very important to understand that every person can live a positive life for the rest of their lives, loving their neighbor, doing that which is good, with the hope that physical life does have existential meaning and purpose and/or that there is a life after death. There is no reason whatsoever to be depressed, there is every reason to do that which is good.

Because it is so easy to misunderstand what we have said, and because even if you understand it goes against human nature to accept, we need to emphasize that the *nothing* we describe cannot lead to depression or fear, or any negative thought or emotion. It is very important to recognize that nihilism can never lead to suicide, for nihilism tells us that if we do in fact live in a nihilistic world, not one thing that happens in our lives, no matter how badly we may feel about it at the time, has any "real" consequence at all. It tells us that if a nihilistic fate awaits us, what we perceive to be the most painful events in our lives are no better, or worse, than any other events. No argument can be made that living with the belief that we face a nihilistic end can ever be logical, rational, or intellectually acceptable.

The possibility of *nothing* leaves you absolutely free to live a life filled with both pain and joy, knowing that if you live in a meaningless world the pain will be as if it never was. Terminating life never brings peace, rather it destroys the possibility of a meaningful, perhaps joyful, existential or non-physical life. We are absolutely convinced that the philosophical neutrality that nihilism and *nothing* demand, means that nihilism never suggests or supports suicide as an option for any human being. If you believe that suicide is an option, you totally misunderstand what you have read, you do not comprehend what it means to say that *nothing* may consume your past, present, and future.

There is no reason at all to reject the possibility that each of us has some kind of permanent physical or non-physical consciousness. There is no reason at all to reject the possibility that each of our lives may have existential meaning and purpose even if there is no life after death. There is no reason whatsoever not to search for an alternative to nihilism, to explore the possibility of a permanent physical or non-physical consciousness, to seek existential meaning and purpose in our lives, to search for a reason for living. There is absolutely no reason whatsoever not to live for the possibility, however remote you may believe it to be, that you can make choices now that will lead you to a positive life that has meaning and value.

If your mind is not receptive and clear, when you read our ideas they may touch raw nerves, and you may stop understanding what we are saying. If you do not agree that the possibility of *nothing* absolutely eliminates suicide as an option then carefully reread our book, including The Possibility of Nothing and this chapter, until you understand why our conclusion is true. No matter what you may think right now, if there is a life after death or if there is no life after death, there is always a possibility that sometime in the future you will find meaning and purpose in your life.

We have readers who indicate that they are distressed and depressed by the possibility that they may have committed the eternal sin. If God exists and if there is an eternal sin, then God gives us the choice to commit the eternal sin or not to commit the eternal sin, period. It would seem that those who have not committed the eternal sin would be distressed if they believed that they might have committed the eternal sin. It would seem that the very fact that someone is distressed by the belief that they may have committed the eternal sin may suggest that they have in fact not committed the eternal sin (we discuss fear of committing the eternal sin in more detail in the Appendix to our LifeNotes book – www.ws5.com).

The following paragraphs contain links to websites which offer information about, and help for, Distress and Depression.

Some who are deeply depressed believe that their lives are meaningless, and to escape the pain of living they seek the peace of suicide. If you are suicidal call the

National Suicide Prevention Hotline 1-800-273-8255

and get professional help immediately.

After that you may want to visit http://www.areason.org and the:

Mental Health Association website

http://www.mentalhealthamerica.net/go/suicide   which includes the following:

"Life is full of good times and bad, of happiness and sorrow. But when you are feeling 'down' for more than a few weeks or you have difficulty functioning in daily life, you may be suffering from a common, yet serious medical illness - called clinical depression.

You are not alone. Every year more than 19 million American Adults suffer from clinical depression. Young or old, man or woman, regardless of race or income - anyone can experience clinical depression. Depression can cause people to lose the pleasure from daily life. It can complicate other medical conditions - it can be serious enough to lead to suicide. Yet this suffering is unnecessary. Clinical depression is a very treatable medical illness. So why don't many people seek the help they need? Clinical depression often goes untreated because people don't recognize the many symptoms. They may know some symptoms, such as sadness and withdrawal, but they are unaware of others, including anxiety, irritability, and sleeplessness. Some incorrectly believe that only people whose depression lasts for months, or who have completely lost their ability to function, have 'real' - or 'clinical' - depression. Many people even wrongly think that depression is 'normal' for older people, young adults, new mothers, menopausal women, or those with a chronic illness. The truth is, clinical depression is never 'normal,' no matter what your age or life situation. Also, people need to know that treatment for clinical depression really works - and to learn how to go about finding the treatment they need.

Clinical Depression can be Successfully Treated

Clinical depression is one of the most treatable of all medical illnesses. In fact, more than 80 percent of people with depression can be treated successfully with medication, psychotherapy or a combination of both. Only a qualified health professional can determine if someone has clinical depression. But knowing the symptoms of clinical depression can help you as you talk with your health professional.

As with many illnesses, if treatment if needed, the earlier it begins, the more effective it can be. And, early treatment increases the likelihood of preventing serious recurrences.

You Do Not Have to Cope with Clinical Depression on Your Own

Some people are embarrassed to get help for depression, or they are reluctant to talk about how they are feeling. Others believe that depression will go away on its own. You can't just 'Tough it out!' Help is available.

Talking to friends, family members and clergy can often give people the support needed when going through life's difficult times. For those with clinical depression such support is important, but it is not a substitute for the care of a health professional. Remember, clinical depression is a serious illness that you do not have to treat on your own."

Depression

The National Institute of Mental Health
http://www.nlm.nih.gov/medlineplus/depression.html offers the following:

"A depressive disorder is an illness that involves the body, mood, and thoughts. It affects the way a person eats and sleeps, the way one feels about oneself, and the way one thinks about things. A depressive disorder is not the same as a passing blue mood. It is not a sign of personal weakness or a condition that can be willed or wished away. People with a depressive illness cannot merely 'pull themselves together' and get better. Without treatment, symptoms can last for weeks, months, or years. Appropriate treatment, however, can help most people who suffer from depression."

Videos

American Museum of Natural History, Isaac Asimov Memorial Debates. "The Existence of Nothing," 2013. http://www.amnh.org/, https://youtu.be/1OLz6uUuMp8

We hesitate to recommend clips from the movie What the Bleep Do We Know because the movie was produced by a Scientology like new age "cult" and had universally bad reviews. The full movie "Down the Rabbit Hole" has too many unsupported claims, and should only be watched by discerning skeptics with science backgrounds, however these clips are concise, entertaining, and basically correct:

Dr. Quantum - Double Slit Experiment https://vimeo.com/109295025

Dr. Quantum - Quantum Entanglement https://vimeo.com/108956253

Dr. Quantum - Flatland https://vimeo.com/108835396

GCSE Science Revision. "Types of Waves," 2005. YouTube video. https://youtu.be/w2s2fZr8sqQ

Greene, Brian. Ted Talk. "Why is Our Universe Fine-Tuned for Life?" - https://youtu.be/bf7BXwVeyWw

Scientific American Video. "Is Our Universe a Hologram?" - https://youtu.be/gS3KWoO9yYA

Scientific American Video. "What is the Wave Function?" - https://youtu.be/aowYf44gDRY

Orzel, Chad. "Particles and Waves: The Central Mystery of Quantum Mechanics?" YouTube Video, 2014: https://youtu.be/Hk3fgjHNQ2Q

Orzel, Chad. "Einstein's Brilliant Mistake: Entangled States," YouTube video., 2014. https://youtu.be/DbbWx2COU0E

Orzel, Chad. "What is the Heisenberg Uncertainty Principle?" YouTube Video, 2014: https://youtu.be/TQKELOE9eY4

Penrose, Roger. "Penrose talks about when we need to sidestep reason." YouTube video., 2008. https://youtu.be/xiYDc1LA0I4

* * * * * * * * * *

Comments to Comments@ws5.com   **[V2]**